PUBLIC NUISANCES

PUBLIC NUISANCES

R. Emmett Tyrrell, Jr.

Drawings by Elliott Banfield

Basic Books, Inc., Publishers   New York

Library of Congress Cataloging in Publication Data

Tyrrell, R Emmett.
    Public nuisances.

    Includes index.
    1. United States—Biography—Anecdotes,
facetiae, satire, etc.   2. Biography—20th century—
Anecdotes, facetiae, satire, etc.   I. Title.
CT120.T96   920'.073   78–19940
ISBN: 0-465-06772-7

To Malcolm and Kitty, Judy and Baron

June 27, 1975
Robertsbridge, Sussex

Be careful too that the reading of your story makes the melancholy laugh and the merry laugh louder; that the simpleton is not confused . . . . In short, keep your aim steadily fixed on overthrowing the ill-based fabric of these books of chivalry, abhorred by so many yet praised by so many more; for if you achieve that, you will have achieved no small thing.

Miguel de Cervantes Saavedra
from *The Adventures of Don Quixote*

Contents

vii

Contents

PART III
THE PUBLIC NUISANCE AS POLITICIAN

PUBLIC NUISANCES

Introduction:
The Art of the Obit

THE AMERICA of the first few decades of this century I have always beheld with horror. The Christian wowser, the prehensile husbandman, the small-town boomer sickened me. Visions of trashy pols and block-headed ministers united in sniffing out every vestige of civilization left in the Republic made the era a gloomy one in my mind. When I read of the life of William Jennings Bryan, I was glad that the intolerant and mischievous old ranter had died, and I rejoiced when I read of how ignominiously he had passed on. The sense that since those times America has steadily improved, becoming ever freer and more congenial to civilization, pleased me and fortified me with a faith that progress means something more than formica, fast food, and mental health associations. In a word, I looked to the liberals in the early 1960s and I was grateful. Some of them were a bit too oleaginous, and the handwringers among them alarmed me, but on the whole they had convinced me that they were my benefactors. I could trust them to ensure freedom, to respect reason, to provide prosperity, and to protect the arts and the Constitution. I was optimistic.

When in the late 1960s the Republic began to rumble, I felt no alarm. The land was full of universities. We would debate, but we would not destroy. We would question, but we would not shout. We would reform, but we would respect reason and the rights of others. Beliefs like these could get one killed by the early 1970s, and I am glad that I caught on fast. By the 1970s America had again become rampant with intolerance, zealous reformers, ignoramuses, and quacks of the most unappealing sort. The liberals had all but disappeared. Some took to calling themselves "radicals" and using exotic herbal soaps. Alger Hiss became a matter of faith once again. A simian beat replaced baroque chamber music. It was everyone for himself. Somehow American liberalism had metamorphosed in the most astonishing way. The public philosophy that had informed us with its discriminating intelligence and elevated values underwent a juvenescence. The capacity to discriminate was lost; the values grew from hideous to childish; the thing became a hollow sham.

America was afflicted with not one Bryan but with multitudes. What is more, they specialized. Some called themselves environmentalists, some feminists, some consumerists. Still others specialized in education, business, national defense, race relations, and so forth. When the Vietnam war ended many of the doves took note of the gorgeous new possibilities for charlatanry, and without hesitating or even blushing they leaped upon the self-improvement and personal development movements. What was worse, these quacks and wowsers were prospering not in the boondocks but in the universities and wherever the university was influential. Bryan advancing on the dirty-necked of backwoods Tennessee had no easier time of it than Ralph Nader or Betty Friedan advancing on Berkeley or Scarsdale.

To my liberal mentors who still clung to the faith, it was a distressing time. They thought they had wiped out the American philistine in his small-town lair, but they now saw the same ignoramuses cleaned up and perfumed and doing very handsomely in the realms of the cosmopolitans. The empty sonorities of such worthies as George McGovern and Jerry Ford were to be expected, but such gibberish was not expected from the so-called educated. Primitive fears and monomanias were associated with hill apes, not with sophisticates. Bringing civilization to the Methodists of the 1920s had been an arduous and uncertain task, for the Methodists had God on their side. But civilizing the intellectualoids of the 1970s would be a monumental undertaking, for they had the Enlightenment plus moral superiority. Today one can listen to the public discourse for days and hear not one sensible thought or even one that avoids clamorous inconsistency. Our eminentoes will say anything and only the criminal code seems to fetter their behavior. In the case of the politicoes, not even the criminal code restrains them. It seems to be an unstated axiom of American life that certain of the eminent among us are never to be held responsible for their actions or utterances. No wonder it appears that the Republic fills with drunks. The governor of California proudly declares that if he could avail himself of the wisdom of any three men he would call upon Irving Kristol, Daniel Patrick Moynihan, and Mao Tse-tung, and still no one gives him an F for being a booby. Rather, the quotation is cited as evidence of an inscrutably capacious mind. Utter nonsense has become the current wisdom.

In my judgment the explication and analysis of all this hokum defy the capacities of the established literary forms. The poem is too ethereal, and its reputation with the scholars too dubious. The essay is too confining. Even the novel fails, and at any rate it seems today to be almost wholly monopolized by fourth-rate females, stuck on the proposition that genital friction is at once epistemologically enlightening and a path to good government. Graffiti does not go far enough. The one literary form that I have found both sufficiently concrete and congenial to speculative thought today is a form curiously shunned by belletrists, though in every newspaper it attracts a larger, more eager readership than the editorial page. As I see it, the literary form most applicable to our time is the obituary.

Admittedly, the obituary has its limitations, for any subject one might wish to eulogize at a given time has to fulfill certain rigid pathological standards about which editors are unusually adamant. Further, when a desirable subject does meet these standards the author is often in no condition to write. For instance, he may be in mourning and despair; then again he may be rejoicing and partaking of the professional services of a favored saloon keeper.

All this having been said, the obituary remains the art form most likely to rouse my afflatus. Moreover, I contend that if the obituary were to gain acceptance with serious writers the commonweal would be enormously improved. Think of how much more decorously our public figures would behave if they lived with the knowledge that, minutes after they had assumed room temperature, every Balzac in the Republic might be furiously tapping out obits not merely for the *popolo minuto* but also for the *culturati*. It would be a different kettle of fish to be sure, and with all this creativity being lavished on the lowly obituary I believe it would grow in complexity and beauty much the way the symphony developed under the nudgings of W. A. Mozart and L. van Beethoven.

Consider, for instance, how differently Senator George McGovern's act might be were he aware that on the day he

6

tripped headlong into his eternal reward an army of writers would be dreaming of their date with the Pulitzer Committee, having written such arty stuff as:

"Senator George S. McGovern passed away early this morning after a restless night, during which he shouted hundreds of thousands of words from speeches he had given throughout his long political career. The end came clamorously as he began going through his famous 'The Sky is Falling' speeches, speeches generally associated with his historically fruitless presidential campaign. His wife told reporters this morning that the distinguished senator had just broken into that famous cadenza of 'Come Home America' exhortations when, as she put it, 'I heard a gurgle and switched on the light just in time to glimpse that look of earnest heroism so familiar to his audiences. Then it faded from his face, to be replaced by the blank look of perfect innocence that he always wore during briefings with his aides and while watching educational television. He had conked, man. It was so characteristic.'

"Indeed it was, Mrs. McGovern. The senator was widely known to be the most gullible man to enter public life since William Jennings Bryan. He would believe anything. Even the nocturnal haranguing was characteristic, for he was a nonstop haranguer. He harangued Americans every day of his long career, and all Washington knew he spouted the same witless sonorities in his sleep that he intoned on the floor of the Senate. He actually believed these flaming exhortations, and early this morning it appears that the cumulative significance of all those monstrous testimonials suddenly burst across his mind's eye. It was too much. Doctors report he died of a massive coronary brought on by fright.

"I do not mean to imply that this gullible blatherskite was simply a dupe. He had his own grand design, but he would

7

believe any idiotic canard that would make that design appear feasible and exigent for America. Eventually he took on more horror stories than his frail constitution could bear.

"What he hoped to achieve in his lifetime was government control over every detail of every American's life. He simply never trusted his fellows, and he lived in constant fear that they would do something horrible. What is more, he believed anyone who claimed that Americans were doing horrible things.

"Oh, those Americans who were drowsing in poverty did not worry him. But give the Americano something to jingle in his pockets, give him some responsibility or some respectability, and Senator McGovern was in a fury to tie him down. Because he feared that free men were capable of any infamy, he confected a rattletrap system of government control, and because he needed to make this absurd system appear plausible, he sought out paragons with which to dazzle us. He raised up one penurious despotism after another for our edification, and whether we nodded in appreciation or not, Senator McGovern bellowed for legislation that would render the American citizenry secure and manageable. His last days were spent in contemplation of the prodigies wrought by Dr. Fidel Castro. The absence of traffic snarls in downtown Havana obsessed him. His ideas were not unlike those of Mother Gandhi, and I have always suspected that had he won the presidency he surely would have visited us with her political system. Nevertheless, the comparison ends with ideology; with intelligence the contrast begins. Senator McGovern was a hopeless dullard. That he once earned a Ph.D. in history was a source of unease at every meeting of the Organization of American Historians.

"Still, his orations and misadventures never ceased to amuse. He could never get into the White House, and as the years wore on his oratory became more desperate and lunatic. An undertone of meanness crept in as it began to dawn on him that the world was passing him by, but since he was utterly without power the meanness only served to make him more absurd and entertaining. I shall miss him."

Thus would I commemorate one of the Senate's leading pests, and the world would be doubtless much improved by such a sendoff. Potential McGoverns would take notice and the Senate would sober up. Much the same therapy could be worked in other areas overpopulated by the obnoxious. Personally I yearn to eulogize freshly departed rock virtuosi, jet set professors, and philistine business tycoons, to name but a few. Let their hearts sputter and pop to a halt, let their juices cool for but a minute, and instantly I would be driving my faithful Olivetti Lexikon 82 to the limit.

Consider this. A rock star, who has been a nuisance for well over a decade, has just exhaled his last pollutant, and the *Times* publishes my obit!

"Internationally acclaimed rock star John Lennon died today at the age of thirty-eight. Death was attributed to old age. Mr. Lennon was one of the Beatles, a rock group that wrote and sang songs urging fraternity, equality, and crackpot socialism, though not one of them could ever get along with anyone, and each of them made more money than a Wall Street bond salesman. Mr. Lennon was a nuisance all of his life.

"He lived on a diet of high-intensity vitamins, for he believed that one's body was the domicile of spirits. To kill and devour animals was not only unhealthy and unjust but also a desecration of one's spirits. Mr. Lennon also renounced vegetables, for he claimed that he once heard a cornstalk sob when it was shorn of one of its ears. His pursuit of bodily health occasionally conflicted with his pursuit of mental well-being, for he spent much of his later years ingesting amphetamines, sniffing cocaine, and smoking hashish. How else was he to spend his time?

"He was a constant participant at protest rallies, and since the end of the Vietnam war he nodded through a prolonged melancholy. During his last days he rarely called his broker and even ceased to make threatening calls to his estranged wife, Yo Yo, who lives in London with their unfortunate son, Splendid Horizon. The name seemed like a fine idea some years back, but times have changed, and young Colin, as he now calls himself, will probably not be attending Mr. Lennon's funeral. Mr. Lennon's foul carcass will be cremated in an outdoor ceremony to be held at Stonehenge. The ceremony will be open to his fans. I hope the rocks fall on them. Good riddance to another 1960s gasbag."

And how I long to publish this one:

"Retired Harvard professor John Kenneth Galbraith died last week en route to Gstaad, Switzerland, where the renowned proponent of socialism usually wintered amid herds of parasitic European aristocrats, movie idols, and Arab real-estate agents. Professor Galbraith wrote twenty books, none of which betrayed a moment of scholarship. His popularity initially derived from his maniac energies and from the fact that he was practically the only American economist who could actually write intelligible English. His sentences were elegant, but his books made no economic sense at all. They never were used by serious economists, though they sold successfully—mainly to readers who admired short titles or who had seen the orotund professor spin his yarns on late-night television shows. At universities they were chiefly used in introductory American history courses, American historians being notorious for their economic benightedness.

Introduction: The Art of the Obit

"Professor Galbraith distinguished himself for being elegantly wrong on practically every issue of the day. In 1968 (on February 15), he announced that the South Vietnamese government would fall 'within the next few weeks.' In the summer of 1975 he augustly declared that if New York City only had some more money its problems would be over. Nevertheless, because of the extraordinary velocity of his pronunciamentoes, people generally forgot his earlier gaffes. Professor Galbraith was a superb example of those frenetic quacks whose doctrinaire nostrums contribute so much to the economic and social problems they claim to be solving. He was a lifelong charlatan, and it is suggestive of the trashiness of our times that he prospered gorgeously."

Finally, though I have only sketched one, I should like to write an obituary about the characteristic capitalist genius who unwittingly makes a huge fortune and then immures himself in a refurbished medieval castle somewhere, venturing out solely to make more money and to act in such a way as to discredit democracy, capitalism, and the human race. Generally he specializes in offending people. He manifests his public-spiritedness by maintaining useless shrines, such as extensive formal gardens featuring rare and poisonous plants. He may be interested in some form of art, but he has almost no interest in the anatomy of the political, economic, or social system. In the unlikely event that he does have some understanding of the culture, he will lift not a finger to support it. To the contrary, he is then apt to donate an incredible sum to an organization dedicated to the destruction of the culture, for he duly suspects any system that has allowed him any room in which to operate. If he has any concern at all for his fellow men it is for the admiration of his enemies. They, of course, loathe him. When he dies, his only monument is a horde of bewildered groundskeepers and domestics. If his family does not immediately squander his wealth, his family and his foundations drain it into useless organizations or groups that are actually subversive. He is the best argument I know for democratic socialism, and before we are stranded in that particular form of government I want to commemorate his achievement.

Unfortunately, the obituary is burdened with still other problems. Most writers, notwithstanding their vaunted iconoclasm, continue to squirm at the thought of death. Then, too, the wonders of American medicine have stretched the life expectancy of public figures to depressing lengths. One cannot even rely on the talents of public-spirited assassins anymore. For a certitude, the Republic abounds with aspirants, but rarely are they devoted to the commonweal. In some advanced societies assassins could be counted on to practice their profession with prudence and dispatch. Even in yesteryear's America, there were assassins who were at least drawn from the higher orders and who displayed education and tact— some emerged from the arts. Alas, today's assassins are more often than not pathetic lunatics roaring with unappealing prejudices: the kind of upper atmosphere liberalism that emanates from National Public Radio. Such addlepated enthusiasts of reform politics as Lee Harvey Oswald, Arthur Bremer, and Citizen Fromme give all assassins a black eye, and anyway they never have the good taste to provide me with the kind of *corpus delicti* I seek to glorify.

Because of all these problems I have been left with an unpublished file of obituaries and brief notes eulogizing the rogues of this legendary epoch, their pernicious ideas, and their preposterous enthusiasms. Now, however, with the increased interest in cultural criticism and recent social history, it has occurred to me that this material might actually have considerable scholarly value. The subjects in my files compose a pointillistic portrait of an especially influential American: the public nuisance. The public nuisance in recent years has obviously become a force to conjure with. On the national scene he turns up everywhere.

I have here assembled a select collection of my obituaries and rid them of their charnal tones, leaving the reader with a more conventional literary form. I have also added a chapter or two of social analysis in the hope of displaying the public nuisance in all his protean destructiveness. My strategy has been to begin with examples of the public nuisance as intellectual, for under that guise he has been particularly influential. I then attempt to explain why the louse element has suddenly been raised to the level of cultural hero, and finally I serve up specimens of the public nuisance in a characteristic role, that of the politician.

Any society that allows its nuisances to rise to such authority does indeed have some underlying problem, but I believe that for the most part American democracy is far sounder than recent critics have allowed. After all, it has responded admirably to many legitimate criticisms raised against it. It has alleviated racial prejudices, aided the poor, and encouraged some tolerance for diversity. It has maintained a modicum of freedom and decency. What it has failed to do is to deal prudently with the violent and idiotic pests who, if they had their way, would undo all this good. In my last chapter I attempt to explain this failure and to prescribe a foolproof cure.

So let us begin with an analysis of the career of Professor Galbraith. We start with him so that you can weigh for yourself the difference between an inspired obituary and a mere essay. But before auspicating the ceremonies, let me pause to thank my staff at *The American Spectator* for covering for me

Public Nuisances

while I was finishing this book. Their devotion and intelligence has allowed much to be accomplished that might otherwise have been aborted. Special thanks is due to Erich Eichman who left his friends Bach and Beethoven to spend many evenings researching this book. Naturally all complaints should duly be directed to him. Testimonials and small cash gifts should be sent to me. And so to Galbraith . . .

PART

I

THE PUBLIC NUISANCE
AS INTELLECTUAL

1

John Kenneth Galbraith:
The Uses of a Wind Instrument

IT IS SUGGESTIVE of the rich times in which we dwell that America's preeminent boomer of socialism, egalitarianism, and an end to hypocrisy in high places, is a millionaire economist and *bon vivant*, an erstwhile Harvard prof who winters in the Alps midst the rich and the powerful. When at home, he upbraids "the Establishment" for an honorarium that would make Norman Thomas blush, occasionally harangues students, and otherwise devotes himself to huckstering flyblown treatises that are snickered at by all serious economists even as they are snatched up as Book-of-the-Month Club selections.

In a time of shifting gullibility and evolving delusions I take the forty-year dance of Dr. John Kenneth Galbraith as solid evidence that you can fool enough of the people enough of the time to make a princely fortune as a public thinker. Had Dr. Galbraith not forsaken an Iona Station, Ontario, dung heap some four decades ago for a cosmetic Ph.D. at Berkeley, the

Public Nuisances

United States would be bereft of one of the most obvious and entertaining mountebanks since Aimee Semple McPherson or Gerald L. K. Smith. This would be a sad loss, for Dr. Galbraith is a stunning exemplification of what Lewis Lapham calls the Great Trick; he has managed to turn himself and all that he discharges into a highly lucrative commodity. Gore Vidal has done it. The pedestrian Warhol has done it. But Galbraith is one of the few academics who have managed it. More than anyone else, Galbraith exemplifies the changed conditions of modern America. The Tennessee rube of yore has been replaced by the demieducated sophisticate. Peruna bows out to Valium and health foods; and the fluent honeyfogler who once worked the hill apes of Arkansas now gets fat and mellow on the earnest intellectualoid. Yesterday's yokel forked up his discretionary income for relief from bodily groans and spiritual fright; the intellectualoid looks to the likes of Dr. Galbraith and so has his fantasies nourished and his soul well greased.

Now to mark Dr. Galbraith down as a mountebank is admittedly to rattle the china, for he is admired by many of the Republic's most eminent minds. Through the years his intellectual circle has included Eugene McCarthy, Arthur M. Schlesinger, Jr., George McGovern, Angie Dickinson; choose your luminary. Practically anyone ever thrown into a Kennedy swimming pool has at one time or another come under Galbraith's spell, and to show him a discourtesy is to play with fire. The old wizard's energies are legendary, and his personal charm brings to mind Beatrice Webb at the height of her powers.

Shortly after his friend and patron, John F. Kennedy, was murdered, Dr. Galbraith made the healing gesture of declaring, "We let the right inject this poison into the American blood stream and this is the result." It is a remark worth re-

18

membering, for it conveys not only Dr. Galbraith's magisterial sense of his own potency, but also his sense of fair play. Moreover, it suggests a major quality of his mind: an ability instantly to abolish truth in the service of the most highly ideologized absurdity.

Think of it, the only evidence available suggested that the assassin was a self-proclaimed Marxist and Castro sympathizer; yet instantly, Dr. Galbraith had grasped what would ultimately become the intellectualoid's solemn belief, to wit: John Kennedy fell to a rightist plot. Instinctively Dr. Galbraith understands how the intellectualoid's mind rebels at mere facts in a rush to embrace the inverted insight. The nature and popularity, today, of the inverted insight I shall discuss anon. That way back in 1963 Dr. Galbraith could manipulate it so smoothly despite sudden tragedy marked him as a man to conjure with.

Immunity to facts and a sure sense of the gullibility of his audience have become characteristic of Dr. Galbraith's work and have made him a rich man. Yet Dr. Galbraith's life has not been all sauce and glory. True, he has made a tidy fortune, but through it all he has had to endure the relentless prejudice and harassment of a dedicated band of small-minded men: the professional economists. Starting with the Keynesians and ending with the Friedmanites, they have all treated him unflatteringly. It is a mark of his incomparable achievement that—though no important economist accepts one of his books or any of his theories—John Kenneth Galbraith stands today as the most widely recognized economist in the country, perhaps the world. He is to economics what Harold Robbins is to the novel. The story of how he overcame the economists' narrow-minded assaults on his scholarship could inspire a whole generation of Clifford Irvings.

Apparently at the outset of his career the economists sought to sink him by a conspiracy of silence, for up to 1952 he was one of the least-discussed scholars laboring at that gloomy science. He had written three books, all of which by his own admission had failed to have any impact at all. Professionally speaking, he was the sound of one hand clapping. But only if you have been in the deepest valley can you ever know how magnificent it is to be on the highest mountain, and Dr. Galbraith now yearned for that mountain. In a manifesto that today takes on great significance he vowed that he "would not be ignored. . . . From now on I would put in an extra year on the writing to engage a larger audience, and because of that the other economists would have to react to me."

What a difference a year makes was shown in his very next book, *American Capitalism: The Concept of Countervailing Power.* It sold tens of thousands. Now the great man had his wider audience. Unfortunately, he had also provoked the economists to react. They hooted him down for claiming that industrial concentrations stimulate the growth of large labor concentrations, and they threw in the *coup de grâce* by pointing to the coal and trucking industries, famous preserves of powerfully concentrated unions. They flayed him for his notion that giant union, giant industry, and giant government all countervail against one another, checking each other's potential abuse of power. It was patently absurd to believe that the three have different interests when, as George Stigler pointed out, all three may very well develop a common interest in fleecing the consumer. What is more, economists already had a mound of evidence demonstrating the inherent wobbliness of cartels. As a piece of economic analysis the thing was fit only for Albanians, but as quackery it was superb.

Publication of *American Capitalism* marked a crucial turning point in Dr. Galbraith's career. He had now arrived as a major American mountebank. The book clearly contained no

research at all, and while the responses of the economists were delayed by their need to test his hypotheses, it became a best seller with those whose ears fill with sirens every time capitalism is the subject of discussion. By the time the economists began stoning him, Dr. Galbraith had assured himself the professorial equivalent of the guaranteed income; the book had made the bibliographies of introductory social-science courses everywhere. The lesson was not lost on the great man, and from that point on, not one of his books would be enfeebled by documentation.

The bombardment that Dr. Galbraith has endured from the Republic's economics departments is eminently well deserved, but often Adam Smith's progeny grow unruly, dismissing him as the Lysenko of economics and resorting to ribaldry too coarse to quote to nonacademic company. Here they go too far, for Dr. Galbraith's habits of ignoring facts and delivering up unsupportable asseverations have constituted a very positive contribution to the study of economics. In attracting mobs of outraged economists he has stimulated a huge amount of scholarship. This was notably the case with *The Affluent Society*—where he ascribed mysterious powers of enchantment to advertising. According to Dr. Galbraith, the Madison Avenue magnificoes were enslaving millions of grown men and women into making purchases that were useless and at times even injurious. The book received exuberant praise from his fans amongst the congenitally fearful, but when economists examined his claims they discovered advertising to be virgin territory. *Hesto Presto*, Dr. Galbraith had opened fantastic research opportunities for hundreds of young scholars. True, their research has almost always found his conclusions doltish, but in mankind's struggle up from darkness no contribution is to be sniffed at.

Further, the economists fail to appreciate the clarity and mellifluence of his prose. Perhaps this is because they almost all write as though plain English were a foreign medium capable of causing bodily harm, but when they read Dr. Galbraith they ought to take notice. He is one of the most elegant writers now manipulating the English language. His 1969 book, *The New Industrial State,* superbly illustrates my point: its publication set the profs to carping that it was idiotic, contradictory of his nonsense in *American Capitalism,* and no closer to the truth. John Jewkes complained that "nearly all the systematic evidence has run counter to it." Harold Demsetz demonstrated that its statement that large corporations sacrifice profits for large sales was unsupportable; that its claim that defense suppliers control their futures through their connections with government was ludicrous; and that its assertion that corporations use their control of prices, advertising, and government intervention to lead trouble-free lives was again unsupportable. Economists as different as Sir Frank McFadzean and Robert Solow were merciless and their minds were not changed when Charles Reich joined in the book's defense. One can imagine the glaze falling over Dr. Galbraith's eyes as he was notified of Charlie's revelation that *The New Industrial State* "changed my life." Charlie was then a leading theorist for the back-to-the-womb movement.

On purely economic grounds *The New Industrial State* was indeed tommyrot but as a piece of poetry it was lovely stuff, full of memorable lines about the "technostructure" and "the pathologically romantic." In it Dr. Galbraith displayed not only his ability to render beautiful the eminently preposterous but also his talent for comedy. In fact, Dr. Galbraith is an accomplished *farceur.* And he is especially funny when dealing with the likes of Friedrich Hayek, Milton Friedman, or for that matter almost any intelligent writer or idea. Whether he is trying to be droll or innocently relating the opposition's ideas as he understands them is an issue over which men of goodwill may differ. As far as I can judge, his humorous treatment of other people's intelligence is intentional, for it is characteristic of a truly great American mountebank to be able to run arpeggios across the whole range of human emotions. His woeful tirades about the injustices of the American system could move the faces of Mount Rushmore to weep, his exposés of the Wall Street mafia could arouse fires of righteous indignation in Oscar Wilde, and his innumerable variations on the theme of nineteenth-century residues in Friedmanite economics still bring a chuckle from Dr. Galbraith's skiing partner, William Buckley, though Buckley has been hearing the joke in its original version for thirty years.

There is a genuine elegance in Dr. Galbraith's mountebankery. Consider the major theme of *The Affluent Society*: our alleged "private opulence and public squalor."* The sonorous terms and their juxtaposition are so lovely as to lull a gout-ridden captain of industry into momentarily forgetting—even in April—that the impoverished public sector which Dr. Galbraith laments has fattened up handsomely since 1929. Then it munched but 10 percent of the Gross National Product; today it chomps down on over 40 percent of the GNP and smacks its lips between yells for the rest. Incidentally, only a

---

* This is not to say that the idea or even the juxtaposition is original. My agents have discovered a long and noble ancestry for this particular line: Tawney, *The Acquisitive Society*, p. 70: ". . . the combination of luxury and squalor." C. F. Masterman, *The Condition of England*, 1909, p. 24: ". . . public penury, private ostentation." Matthew Arnold, *Culture and Anarchy*, 1891, p. 20: "London, with its unutterable external hideousness, and with its internal canker of *publice egestas, privatim opulentia*—to use the words which Sallust puts into Cato's mouth about Rome—unequalled in the world." Soame Jenyns, *Thoughts on High Prices*, 1767, p. 27: the sorrows of his day were due to "private wealth and public poverty."

few years after Dr. Galbraith did so well off his disquisition on the affluent society he did even better with the war on poverty. That war might not have done much for the disadvantaged, but it greatly enlarged and enriched Dr. Galbraith's audience, creating lush opportunities for thousands of social workers, social scientists, and other prospective customers of the Galbraithian bunk.

Dr. Galbraith's acuity in adapting his spiel to changing enthusiasms has now been baldly displayed in the third edition of *The Affluent Society*. When the first edition appeared, egalitarianism fevered only a handful of America's left-wing dreamers, and so Dr. Galbraith's treatment of it was brief, suggesting in fact a steady trend toward equality. By the third edition his customers had grown addicted to the egalitarian moonshine, lost in the conviction that America harbored ever wider economic disparities. Dr. Galbraith's response was to mix up a potion that would sell. In his first edition he states that the poorest 10 percent of families and unattached individuals "received after taxes about one percent of the total money incomes," and the top 10 percent of American incomes "averaged 27 times as much as the lowest tenth." In the third edition he updates these figures and finds himself in a pickle, for there has been considerable equalization between top and bottom income groups. Even the slippery statistics he resorts to show as much. The lowest tenth now receives "2 percent" of the total money incomes and the top 10 percent now averages only "14 times" as much as the bottommost, and this is no longer "after taxes" but "before taxes." Hence, to keep his readers buying, not only does he dissemble by ignoring the trend toward equality, but he actually slips in a sentence calculated to inflame them: "It is only necessary to observe that for many years no serious effort has been made to alter the present distribution of income." Furthermore he has deleted from the third edition certain incriminating charts, which reveal significant equalization in the first half of this century.

Now the sheer fecundity of Dr. Galbraith's nonsense has provoked many scholars to ruminate over his intellectual origins. The arrogance, the paternalism, the contempt for ordinary people, the reliance on ipsedixitisms regardless of their factual ricketiness, and the statism have inspired some to identify him as a child of nineteenth-century Tory Radicalism. This judgment seems far off the mark. On the basis of the evils he has discoursed upon in his books, one clearly sees that he is a typically American hayseed mountebank retooled for a modern audience. That is to say, he is a haranguer full of hatred for sound money, Eastern bankers, big business, the diversity and progress of a free society, and the dynamism and easy skepticism of urban life. His apparent arrogance might be more accurately perceived as a pride in one's own inferior prejudices. No Arkansas cracker was ever more smug about his belief in the Good Book and the mule than Galbraith is about his imbecile stew of Marx, Thorstein Veblen, and a half-baked Keynesianism. To find Galbraith's antecedents one need not look to the grave of some aristocratic British philosopher. Look to Cotton Ed Smith standing midst the dust and horseflies of some jerkwater metropolis, terrorizing the credulous with tales of the evils of Shylock bankers and indoor plumbing. Or look to Gerald L. K. Smith. Until Smith drew his last greedy breath he dreamt of a peasants' army of Christian morons marching out of Oklahoma, advancing gloriously on the delicatessens and libraries of New York. Galbraith beholds mechanized divisions, revving up their Volkswagens and Volvos and roaring out of all the college towns of America; Luddite sophomores encircling New York, Chicago, and Los Angeles, closing forever the messy factories, destroying the banks. Advertising executives will be guillotined immediately, and the jails will bulge with every wealthy American not working for the Department of Health, Education and Welfare and related industries. There you have Dr. Galbraith's antecedents. That they were all grasping yahoos is amusing. That they have all been inimical to freedom is a matter of record.

2

Lillian Hellman:
Triumph of a Schoolgirl

I CANNOT and will not cut my conscience to fit this year's fashions"—proud and worthy words, declaimed in the cruel spring of 1952 as mobs of American Legionnaires swept down the boulevards of America and the virtuous remnant shivered behind drawn curtains, schooling themselves in the legal arcanum of the Fifth Amendment: "I refuse to answer on the grounds, I refuse to answer on the grounds. . . ." The fever of McCarthyism was upon the Great Republic: the Bill of Rights had been adjourned, the Supreme Court was in hiding, every cultural fount in the Republic was being patrolled by fanatical yahoos and—worse still—arrant anti-Communists. Why Miss Lillian Hellman, the ageless coed who intoned the above declaration of principle, was not immediately arrested and garroted at the feet of the Statue of Liberty is a mystery. How the Republic survived into the present is a greater mystery still. Yet Miss Hellman is here with us today, free to relate this tale of villainy, fain to admit her dominant role in saving us from the totalitarian night, and glad to fill her purse with loot so suavely exacted from that vast body of untutorable gulls who today queue up for every sequel of anti-American soap opera provided by Hollywood and the publishing industry.

Lillian Hellman is an enduring example of those self-obsessed Americans who derive such vast moral satisfaction from reassuring America's international critics that life in the Great Democracy is not such a pretty picture. During the 1970s hysteria over the 1950s hysteria, she became a cult figure—her doddering, self-congratulatory figure greatly in demand at those fatuous extravaganzas where moral superiority is the rallying point even as Gucci, Pucci, and Cucci are the costumers.

Nowhere can the absurdity of the woman be more vividly seen than in her 1976 literary sensation, *Scoundrel Time*. There she chronicled her life in the American Gulag, a subtle kind of prison perhaps but a prison made all the more pervasive and heinous by its very lack of bars, guards, and material deprivation. Democracy is the cruelest imprisonment of all.

Billed as a memoir, *Scoundrel Time* was, in its vitals, the balmy diary of a spoony schoolgirl. Were we inhabiting any other era, one might imagine that a mischievous brother had plucked Lillian's torrid manuscript from its hiding place beneath a tangle of teen-form bras and smuggled it off to a publisher of fourth-rate melodrama. But these are great days. The intellectualoids yearn for tales of 100 percent American infamy, and the ancient laws of supply and demand respond unhesitatingly. Hence, for a pittance, readers of *Scoundrel Time* can gasp with Lillian Hellman, the sempiternal college girl lost in trivial and incoherent fantasies, self-pitying, self-deluding, and mortifying. Lillian is flaming youth, an ingenue ill-used by this too, too cruel world and often am-

29

bushed by the uncontrollable thumpings of her very big heart. Great fame exacts its toll. Genius is abused and betrayed. Life is hard. Nonetheless the kid bounces back: she is a trooper, an intellect of note, a good and indomitable spirit. How she has suffered! How any literate person who has to indulge her maunderings will suffer! If *Scoundrel Time* had been written by Shirley Temple Black the chichi intelligentsia would still be larfing; because it was written by a 100 percent anti-American it was taken as very solemn stuff. Lillian Hellman is to our era what Patty Hearst might become. Whether Patty ever has her diary published is a question of moment to lovers of literature everywhere, but for now we have to satisfy ourselves with the adventures of Lillian.

As with all diaries, *Scoundrel Time* is elliptical, a concatenation of events and insights of quality varying from the pedestrian to the moronic. Yet the thing is sustained by the almost voluptuous attraction of Lillian's incessant bellyaching about how a conspiracy of right-wing pols and left-wing intellectuals denied her a $140,000-a-year honorarium for creating Hollywood masterpieces. Such a complaint issuing from Lillian has great dramatic force, though she has a Mongolian's ear for English prose and no regard for historical accuracy whatsoever.

You see, Lillian is no champion of the Chamber of Commerce—much the contrary. She is an artiste and lifelong critic of George Babbitt, all he stood for, and all his bourgeois kin. This notwithstanding, she loved that $140,000-a-year income; and I am personally relieved to see that the capitalists have held no grudges. According to the authoritative *Publishers Weekly* she now maintains well-appointed quarters overlooking Park Avenue and a house on Martha's Vineyard—all the better to continue her researches into the evils of America's privileged classes. What is more, the Blackglama fur company

Lillian Hellman

has given her a $7,000 mink coat for modeling it for the *New Yorker*—another example of capitalism's brazen exploitations perhaps, but a swell mink coat nonetheless.

Born of wealthy and somewhat moldy New Orleans parents, Lillian allowed Mr. and Mrs. Hellman to escape what must have been a life of hell when she took her marvelous mind and all of its complaints off to New York, there to study at New York University, drop in on the highbrow salons, and pick up the visionary notions of the young Trotskyites without ever having to read Trotsky or accept an ice axe to the cerebrum. In the 1930s she became a playwright of third-rate stuff and a rising Hollywood dramatist. But always she returned to Dashiell Hammett, a modern Dickens whose reverence for the brotherhood of man compelled him to side with Marshal Joseph Stalin, the late Soviet humanitarian.

Dash and his friends never broke with the enlightened Russian. They stuck with him through the Moscow trials, the purges, the Hitler pact, the whole program of reform and Soviet uplift. If Lillian did not approve such cosmopolitan associations it is one of the few complaints she has ever kept to herself. In fact, to this day she remains somewhat coy about Old Joe, referring to his torture chambers, his concentration camps, and his show trials as "infringements on personal liberty." At the same time she railed lustily against anti-Communist liberals like John Dewey and Sidney Hook, who challenged the fairness of the Moscow trials. Moreover, she published these objurgations in cultural journals like the *Daily Worker* and *New Masses*.

During the 1940s when anti-Communists were barred from Hollywood and from university teaching posts, she was off mooning over deer on her upstate New York farm, dreaming of the day when she could fence them all in near her picture window, the better to appreciate their sylvan charm. Henry Wallace's preposterous run for the White House fetched her to the soapbox. Simultaneously she served as his Ron Ziegler and his Rabbi Korff. Wallace repaid her with one poached egg laid upon a shredded wheat biscuit and a fifty-pound bag of manure. Think of it, she hollered for the only presidential candidate in the history of the Republic actually to subscribe to the hocus-pocus of an Asian mystic, the Rev. N. Konstantinovich Roerich, a quack guru for a sect of theosophists! Wallace's party was called the Progressive Party, and it was composed of equal parts Communists and simpletons. How shocked she must have been after the 1948 election, in which the Progressives fared no better than the last-ditch Prohibitionists.

Nevertheless, the indomitable Lillian still burned for a better world, and in 1949 she served as the Shirley MacLaine of the famed Waldorf-Astoria Cultural and Scientific Conference for World Peace—quite possibly the most outlandish collection of Stalinists and fellow travelers ever allowed outside the Soviet Fatherland. For once a spark of idealism flickered in America! The comrades were itching to get down to some constructive lying and utopianizing when in barged that ferocious Communist-hater Norman Cousins, leading an entire brigade of *Saturday Review* storm troopers. It was a grim moment, especially when the fierce Cousins questioned the brethren about their possible allegiances to a "foreign government." Gulps were heard throughout the ballroom, Adam's apples bobbed furiously, but Lillian screwed up her courage and with pith and wit scotched the knave. The conference was saved, but Lillian was to pay for her spunk. God knows how many Hollywood masterworks were lost during her ensuing ordeal.

At the end of World War II, when the devious American government withdrew its armies into occupational zones, reduced its troop strength from 12 million to approximately 1.5 million (within seven months of the war's end), and proposed the international control of atomic power, red stars sprouted throughout Eastern Europe. Our heroic Soviet allies reneged on the Yalta agreement and became dyspeptic over all sorts of diplomatic questions. American military secrets began turning up in Soviet attaché cases, Czechoslovakia was forcibly overthrown, and Lenin's pupils throughout the world began to crow and to fuss. China fell to the poet, Soviet defectors told ghastly tales, and Marshal Sokolovsky blockaded Berlin. The

33

Public Nuisances

Communist North Koreans swarmed into South Korea. Through it all Americans grew increasingly dubious of Communists and downright curious about Lillian's friends. Congressmen started calling them before their investigative committees both to fashion antisubversive legislation and to snare headlines.

Now, to my mind, no congressional committee should ever have the power to demand testimony from reluctant private citizens. If congressmen cannot research legislation in ways that do not infringe on the constitutional liberties of private citizens, they ought not to make such legislation. Citizens suspected of crimes should be prosecuted in courts of law, not persecuted before ambitious congressmen who deny them the legal safeguards of the courtroom.

This having been said I leave it to future generations to decide whether when called before the House Committee on Un-American Activities on May 21, 1952, Lillian acted honorably, intelligently, or even rationally. Her desultory discussion of the epic event in *Scoundrel Time* raises doubts. All we know for a certitude is that before her appearance this defender of the proletariat yearned for steak, caviar, an expensive dress, and the chance "to spend a lot of money on something." She got the dress, scrapped a visit to the National Gallery because there was "no place to walk refined," and instead examined the Washington zoo, for, she apprises readers, "I've always wanted to go to bed with an orangutan." Having made her famous statement to the committee—"I will not cut my conscience to fit this year's fashions"—she sells her New York farm and vamooses to Rome. Behind all these tribulations Lillian sees the dark hand of democracy; however, insofar as I have been able to penetrate her dizzy narrative all I can perceive is Lillian's almost willful naiveté and impudence.

It is characteristic of Lillian to exempt certain relevant matters from her diary—especially when those matters smudge her halo. For instance, it is both illustrative of her predicament and suggestive of her character that many of her friends were not simply Marxists but slavish Stalinists. Further, most of them were making a bundle and continued to do so throughout the 1950s. Close textual analysis of *Scoundrel Time* and of Lillian's earlier biographical recollections convinces me that many of her associates were ignoramuses, others were bitter-end malcontents, while the rest were mostly bounders, catatonic liars, half-wits, CIA prowlers, and the most egregious of Hollywood's wheeler-dealers. If she ever associated with any normal Americanoes other than her domestic servants she never mentions it. It comes as no surprise to me that her political aspirations for humanity were so foolish; had I come from such a jungle my political philosophy might include whopping doses of cannibalism.

Of course, the absurd nature and behavior of her associates are not the only pieces missing from the puzzle Lillian presents. Missing also is any suggestion that in the early 1950s there was ever anyone, aside from Lillian, actively critical of the forms anti-Communism had taken. Lillian never reveals why anti-Communism had such broad support, aside from her bogus explanation that it was a reaction to the New Deal. And she neglects the evidence and reasoning for dozens of other appalling canards such as the claim that "Cold War anti-Communism was perverted . . . into the Vietnam war and then into the reign of Nixon, their [anti-Communists'] unwanted but inevitable leader." Yet the largest piece missing from her diary is a portrait of Old Joe, one of the most bloodthirsty tyrants of all time. Throughout her woeful maunderings Lillian hardly mentions him: the socialist father figure who, by the late 1940s, had already done in some twenty million of his own countrymen, established the horrible Gulag, broken his

Public Nuisances

word on countless diplomatic agreements, and ravished much of Asia and all of Eastern Europe. His agents were at work throughout most of the civilized world, and free citizens everywhere had reason in the wake of Hitlerism to fear Soviet expansion and subversion. Popinjays like Lillian had become nuisances. True, nuisances have their rights, but from Lillian's revelations I cannot see that her fellow Americans abused her all that much. That she howls so about how society battered her and set her down ever so temporarily into the middle class is only evidence that, as nuisances go, Lillian is a decadent nuisance—the prototype for radical chic.

There has arisen in the land a new and prosperous breed of charlatan, the revisionist whose chief racket is merchanting the inverted insight, a colossal bit of intellectual sleight-of-hand that propounds as the truth that which is precisely the opposite of logical deduction and plain fact. There have always been enormous numbers of people whose intellects furiously resist reality, who search out the most remote explanations for the most commonplace happenings, who live with the conviction that influenza and misfortune are always the creation of winged spirits and gyrating heavenly bodies. The modern intellectualoids feast on such preposterous explications, and so they have ravenously gulped down the works of writers like Lillian without even pausing to spit out the seeds. That Lillian's tale is full of poppycock, inconditely prepared by a writer seemingly incapable of the higher forms of cognition, does not even occur to them. They thrill to the obvious inverted insights that "America in the early 1940s fell in love with total war," that Harry Truman "launched the Cold War in the spring of 1947," and that anti-Communist intellectuals of the 1950s conduced America "straight into the Vietnam War and the days of Nixon."

Lillian Hellman

The first two of these whoppers were laid down by Garry Wills in his introduction to *Scoundrel Time,* and they so neatly typify the inverted insight that I would be remiss were I to allow them to pass. The last is sheer Hellman, fraud *supérieure* and heroine to that strutting lout that Vic Gold has labeled the Gucci liberal.

3

Charles Reich:
A Prophet Discarded

THE YEAR was 1977, and the last vestiges of Nixonism were being erased from our nation's capital. A Georgia Democrat—a Bible-pounding Baptist—was president of the Great Republic. A Boston Irishman was Speaker of the House of Representatives. A southerner and former Ku Kluxian reigned supreme as Senate Majority Leader. There were fewer women in the Ninety-fifth Congress than in the Ninety-fourth. There were no women in the Senate. Thus, after a decade of manifestoes, turbulence, prophecy, and prayer, I present to you the long-awaited New Age, the New Politics, the New Consciousness. Finally we can taste the change so fervently fought for by the heroes of the 1960s!

How did such a prodigious metamorphosis occur? One of the New Age's most celebrated prophets spotted the stirrings early, and in 1976 he paused to describe the whole gorgeous process; read carefully: "I saw new consciousness first in Berkeley, California, in the summer of 1967. I saw it more deeply at

Yale, 1967–70. It changed me and changed my life. I remember this as a time of incredible excitement and discovery, of opening up to unknown realms and corridors, lights and colors, undreamed-of places in the mind and the feelings. It had the power of a primal event which had to be accepted with wonder and awe. There was a sense of dawn, of daybreak over the land. Spontaneously, almost accidentally, a large number of people discovered that they could change. They could grow by expanding their minds and opening up to new ways of thinking. Old ways of thinking had become entrenched, obsolete, and finally destructive." So spoke Professor Charles Reich, one of the great heroes of the 1960s, seven years after writing his monumental work, *The Greening of America*. It is a modern classic in cultural forecasting.

What a pother it created. At one time *Greening* was more intensely talked about than the Bible or any sex manual ever written. Perhaps its lucubrations never jolted the unlettered, but it was learnedly dissected on all the talk shows and even Rotarians heard tell of its prophecies. God knows it was potent stuff in Winnetka, Illinois, and how it did invade the universities! True, the Republic's snootier intelligentsia greeted it with a general roll-of-the-eyes, but that did not daunt thousands of university professors from a myriad of disciplines who made it essential reading in their classes. Overnight, crazy Charlie was the new Plato. College girls read him and wept. College boys read him and a squadron of butterflies took off in their tummies. The profs underlined. Then Charlie sank from sight and from mind.

His perfumed and voluptuous visions were not long missed, however, for American culture is colossally fecund nowadays. Today at least as many frauds ply the populace as ever ministered to the boobs of the 1920s, and their snake oil is infinitely more amusing and edifying for they labor amongst the tin-pot intelligentsia. Furthermore, as Charlie's career richly suggests, they fall for their own hocus-pocus, and it foozles them beyond repair. Remember if you can such dizzy transients of recent American history as Dr. Timothy Leary, Dr. Daniel Ellsberg, and the gifted Berrigans. Our era abounds with such overnight luminaries momentarily cashing in on visions of apocalypse and on gimmicky left-wing pontifications.

Perhaps in another time it was the average Americano who was a poltroon and a sap for any fabulist intent on working him over, but times have changed. Today one has a better chance of finding good sense and generous sentiment in the corner barbershop than at practically any cultural redoubt. This is not to say that there are not civilized people to be found amongst the culturati, but such people are assuredly the exception. Those who compose the rule are overwhelmingly idiots adept in the most preposterous hysteria. They fall for tales of terror and images of utopia, and whereas in an earlier era our Charlie would have been given an animal bladder and sent to perform under Mr. Ringling's Big Top, today he or one like him is trumpeted by the great publishing houses and invited to tour the cultural Chautauqua circuit from Harvard to Malibu, California.

Charlie was one of the most formidable clowns ever loosed on the vaguely intellectual. More than one Jaycee gave up his reverence for cash-flow to follow Charlie, and his prognostications of pandemic whoopee were even entered into the *Congressional Record*. Yet the culturati tire, and poor Charlie was soon left high, dry, and ranting. Then, he published his sequel, *The Sorcerer of Bolinas Reef*, from which the above quotation was lifted. *Sorcerer* attracted not a peep of laudation despite the fact that the book was even more thunderingly moronic than *Greening*. In *Sorcerer* Charlie tells us the full story of his discovery of Consciousness III, that sudden uni-

Charles Reich

versal awareness that did so much to finish off bourgeois
America in the late 1960s. In it he foretold even vaster revolu-
tions for America, and he included helpful hints on how the
reader might prepare for life in the forthcoming era. New fore-
casts of drastic social change generally fetch the intelligentsia
even if the forecaster is a has-been. Yet not even the *New York
Review of Books* gave Charlie a nod—an unusual event that,
for this famous review is given to celebrating worthies like
Charlie regardless of their future prospects. It actually keeps
connoisseurs like Dr. Garry Wills and Gore Vidal on retainer
for the sole purpose of whooping it up every time a travesty like
The Sorcerer of Bolinas Reef comes along. How does one explain the silence? It is my judgment that Charlie and his second tome fell to a curious conspiracy, and that Charlie's sad
oblivion tells us much about a subgroup of Americans peculiar to our era and enormously pernicious.

Surely *Sorcerer* was not ignored because Charlie's earlier
celebration of hedonism had slipped so rapidly into the narcis-
sism inhering throughout his second book. Nor was he passed
over because of the book's metaphysical maunderings over
rock music, dope, and John Kenneth Galbraith's *The New Industrial State*, a book he found absolutely crucial to his intellectual development. I even doubt that his 1976 confessions to
a life of pederasty, a belief in magic, and a passion for "cookies
and milk" brought him to his eventual low estate. Such passions are common amongst his circle of readers, though most
were initiated into them in a different sequence than poor
Charlie, who admits to never having experienced any sort of
coition until the gray age of forty-four—two years after the
publishing of *Greening!*—and then only with a "male model"
who charged him $25 and took a $10 gratuity. Women's delights he savored still later.

The truth is, Charlie was blacklisted! I believe he was black-

Public Nuisances

listed because the very boldness and breadth of his last book were simply too much for the left-wing culturati. Most of them devoutly believe in Charlie's personal philosophy of hedonism, self-absorption, and juvenescence; not to do so would be provincial. The left-wing culturati accept a politics that grafts the idealism of Mao Tse-tung to the realism of Eleanor Roosevelt, and most desire that our foreign policy be based on the programs of the New York City Department of Social Services; but few would be so artless or so reckless as to harangue for the whole smash in one book. When Charlie did that he mortified a large number of America's cultural entrepreneurs; moreover, he scared hell out of them.

Charlie is one of those members of today's professional class whose roots reach deep into American liberalism, but whose jejune preferences and political posturings make them paradigmatic members of the New Class. To this rising class of Americans he became an embarrassment; he was a premonitory image of their foolishness. Raised in Manhattan's toney East Eighties by a father and mother who adored the New Deal, Charlie was given his first glimpse of the New Age vision at Oberlin College, where the amplitude of earthly wealth is assumed along with the unimportance of work and the rapacity of capitalism. Full of zeal for reform and a hunger for power, Charlie went to Yale to study law and clerked for Hugo Black. He became a friend and disciple of William O. Douglas, whom he calls "the Sun God himself." Later he practiced with Arnold, Fortas & Porter, the prestigious Washington law bordello that years later employed the likes of Joe Califano. Always Charlie brought energy to his work and saw society as a series of problems to be solved. In the 1960s he began teaching law at Yale. Through all these years he gained no sympathy for the scarcity of economic goods, the fragility of political liberty, or the importance of lives led outside the public sector.

42

In short and in sum, Charlie had access to practically all the benefits chic liberalism could accord a young man—an elite education, access to elite institutions, power, ease, and the *New York Times* with breakfast; by the late 1960s it became apparent to all that the experience had idiotized him. He wrote *Greening,* and gained wide fame. His every word was quoted. And those words were not just moronic; they were pristine ritualistic liberalism. What The Enemy could do to the liberal endeavor if they ever drew this connection! One day Charlie would harangue on behalf of "the kids"; the next day he might air his obsession with Brooks Brothers, whose suits were "scratchy" and "interfered with the free movement of my mind." Worse still was a rhetorical quirk that struck terror in the hearts of his more circumspect fellows. In the midst of the most lunatic discourse he would suddenly gain his composure, clear his throat, and launch a pious declaration along the lines of the following from *Sorcerer* (page 244 for anyone who can still locate the book): "The major goal of my own work is fundamental, political change. I cannot accept living in a country where people feel powerless to affect their lives. I am unwilling to overlook injustice, cruelty, and oppression. I cannot in good conscience live in a country that imprisons people, humiliates them, degrades them, or ignores their basic humanity. I do not want to live in a country where there is such pervasive cynicism, corruption, and betrayal of its own dignity. I want nothing to do with a country that oppresses the people of any other country. Therefore I want to bring down this system, and replace it with one responsive to human needs."

Mein Gott! Such sentiments! This is no mere cultural quack. It is George McGovern on the floor of the U. S. Senate. It is Senator Edward Kennedy discoursing with a Third World mullah. It is an editorial writer for the *Nation* abusing his bartender. If ever the forces of reaction heard such noble

Public Nuisances

statements issuing from our Charlie they would have ammunition enough to destroy the Army of Decency forever. And so poor Charlie was entombed in a conspiracy of silence, a quack undone not only by his own quackery but also by the cowardliness of his erstwhile press agents. As a cultural phenomenon of the late 1970s Charles Reich was at one with the brontosaurus, the pterodactyl, and the Kingston Trio.

Charlie, *au revoir* to you and to your dream. The whole thing would have been beautiful were it not for the fact that our chichi liberals quaver and flinch before the specter of America's Chamber of Commerce.

4

Theodore H. White
and the *Bruit Nouveau*

THE LAST few decades have been harsh ones for book publishers. Radio and television have seduced large numbers of their customers, causing desperation among the tycoons of letters. They publish more porn, but the television screens continue to glow. They publish books to satisfy every primitive fear, but they attract only casual readers. Upper-level management in the great publishing houses inclines away from intelligent writing, and the marketing geniuses agree. Publishers employ ever more PR wizards and pray for scandal with every book they turn out. Nothing would please some of these grim entrepreneurs more than a resurrection of the libel laws and the easy celebrity such laws might allow.

Nevertheless, the electronic media remain impregnable monopolists of America's leisure hours. Simply stated, radio and television provide more cheap thrills. Yet, for nearly twenty years one writer, Theodore H. White, has manfully challenged the electronic monsters. In so doing he has actually developed a new kind of book, one designed to assault the senses as powerfully as any broadcast. His books have become nearly as stentorian as the evening news, and even more senti- mental. At their *ne plus ultra* they equal in luridness and idi- ocy any prime-time sensation. So successfully have White's tomes competed with the broadcast media's noise and fever index that the whole McLuhan canon is again in dispute. Yet the publishers' gain is no gain for readers. White's historical melodramas commit mayhem on the truth and atrocity against intelligence.

Up until now reviewers could write of a book that they could not put down or a book that they would never forget or a book that changed their lives, but now with White's literary breakthrough they can write about a book that will not shut up. In 1975 the White genre reached its efflorescence with *Breach of Faith.* When you purchased that book you pur- chased something more than a best seller—you purchased a mother-in-law. Savor the experience.

You carry it home, and it begins to stir under your arm. In the glow of your reading light it lurches violently, and when you open it you are practically flattened as it roars its first oro- tund sermon and shrieks its first condemnation. Soon it is gushing forth its message. It bellows. It vaticinates. It croons. It is the noisiest book ever printed. Close its cover and it still chatters away. Bury it beneath pillows and it will not relent. Drop it in the bathtub and it hisses, it gurgles, it drones on, in- vincible and unabashed. *Breach of Faith* is literary muzak. It is written for people whose brains disrelish the printed word. It is for the oral maniacs of the present. It shouts at them and they love it. White is one of the most garrulous writers ever un- corked. Next to him Hubert Humphrey could have been a model librarian.

Breach of Faith is White's bombastic rendering of Richard

Nixon's last crisis, Watergate—an American legend already used by thousands of schoolmarms to demonstrate the moral lesson once demonstrated so much more mildly by George Washington's cherry tree imbroglio. White's story begins with RMN hunkering under his desk, hoping against hope that the American people are unable to comprehend plain English when they hear it on tape. Alexander Haig is entreating him to rise to the occasion and scram; over in the Capitol, Peter Rodino, MC, is sobbing; and elsewhere Gerald Ford is furiously burning his entire wardrobe of double-knit suits. Next, White describes recent changes in American life, slipping into a tone reminiscent of Genesis.

Then comes another of those sweeping biographical vignettes, so essential to the White technique. We glimpse RMN struggling up from the log cabin, passing through the searing experience of California politics, treading water as Vice President behind one of the greatest dog-paddlers in American presidential history, and finally the most searing experience of all: a presidential campaign against John F. Kennedy, Lyndon B. Johnson, and a host of Democratic ghosts inhabiting some surprisingly populous cemeteries in Chicago and Texas. In White's hands this political biography takes on the proportions of a saga. It provides us with all sorts of luscious information about RMN, his associates, his adversaries, and his country—everything except an analysis of RMN's peculiar and protean connection with political principle. That White never discusses this in all his verbosity is, of course, to be expected. A careful discussion of anything so complicated as political principle might lose thousands of readers to ABC.

Instead White roars and sobs portentously about the numinous qualities of the presidency and the enormities about to be perpetrated by RMN. By chapter 5 White has us gathered up around him in a fever to find out how all those enormities commenced. Here is how. One of RMN's lowlier staff assistants, Tom Charles Huston, "because he was a favorite of Bob Haldeman, because his ideas had reached the President . . . could sit with the masters of American intelligence, commanding billions of dollars and thousands of agents, and dominate all but one of them, J. Edgar Hoover." There you have it, Tom Charles Huston, Watergate's uncaused cause. It is at moments like this that a White book begins to show its donkey ears. Watergate may, indeed, have been cheap theater, but its historical explication demands something more than the Rex Reed treatment. This is bad journalism and worse history. The simple exegeses of Walter Cronkite might be essential, even unobjectionable, for TV news specials; but readers of books have some advantage over TV viewers. They can stop a commentator in his tracks. They can turn back his pages, reflect on his argument, and verify his facts. What is more, readers of books can make photostats of foolish passages and mail them to the author with suitable recommendations. That Mr. White cannot write carefully about what is obviously one of the most important political events of this century is unfortunate, but then no one since him has done a very good job of it either. In the late 1970s a careful chronicling of Watergate and a sober analysis of its consequences remains to be written.

What White calls the Huston Plan was a plan calling for the restructuring of the American intelligence community and recommending various activities such as surreptitious entry, mail covers and interceptions, the penetration of reputed subversive groups, and the monitoring of international cable traffic. The recommendations had been made to the President through his young White House aide, Huston. The plan went into effect on July 23, 1970, and was withdrawn *five* days later!

Arguably it was an imprudent scheme, but the obsession that it became for some people in the 1970s is suggestive of the asinine posturing so popular during the period.

White's treatment of the legendary plan is typical and instructive. That White can seriously suggest that its author, a twenty-nine-year-old White House transient, "dominated" the chiefs of the Central Intelligence Agency and the National Security Agency would strain the faith of a Boy Scout. Yet in the 1970s America was alive with high-minded and overaged Boy Scouts. And so White could luridly claim that the Huston Plan represented: (1) an ominous turning point in the Nixon administration, (2) a direct route to Watergate, and (3) a "heresy, or truly dangerous thought." No one laughed; instead White's public bought the book and cringed over how close we came to the totalitarian winter. White's readers thrill to these huffings and puffings, and they also love his visual touches. The jacket of a White book has more American eagles and more bunting than a Fourth of July reviewing stand in downtown San Diego. *Breach of Faith* is one of his greatest productions ever. It is draped in covers of gold, silver, blues, and reds. It is engauded with presidential seals, and every conceivable version of the American Eagle. Even by American Legion standards it is a monster. The tome looks like it belongs in the White House and doubtless is meant to add tone to the coffee table of any White addict.

Subsequent to the publication of *Breach of Faith* various government investigations revealed not only that the intelligence chiefs had been free of the duress of Huston but that they had been tolerably free of the influence of several presidents. According to figures made public by the Senate Select Committee on Intelligence on September 25, 1975, the Federal Bureau of Investigation committed at least 238 surreptitious entries from 1942 to 1968. On September 24, 1975, former CIA counterintelligence chief James Angleton testified that his agency had illegally intercepted all mail to and from the Soviet Union from 1952 to 1973. The penetration of groups adjudged subversive is old hat; according to disclosures by the Senate committee on November 6, 1975, international cable traffic was monitored by the National Security Agency from 1947 to May of 1975 without the knowledge of any president since Harry Truman. The fever over the Huston Plan was a simpleton's witchhunt led by Pecksniffs.

Because White's blowsy analysis of Huston and his plan is pivotal to White's analysis of Watergate and the cover-up, it is the most crucial of his misstatements—it is not his last. In fact, viewed with respect to historical accuracy, *Breach of Faith* can be read as a sustained insult to the Organization of American Historians. White's knowledge of the Founding Fathers is almost a case of the inverted insight. As he sees them, James Madison and his associates were indistinguishable from an assemblage of Rexford G. Tugwells. According to the author: (1) "What he [RMN] did not understand was the past—or the reasons why Americans so long ago had originally put so much potential power in the office he held. . . . he had broken with the faith that had glued Americans to each other in the beginning to make a republic"; (2) "Of all the political myths out of which the republic was born . . . none was more helpful than the crowning myth of the presidency—that the people, in their shared wisdom, would be able to choose the best man to lead them"; (3) ". . . the presidency, the supreme office, would make noble any man who held its responsibility." Such balderdash is characteristic of White. At one point in *Breach of Faith* he erases from the record practically every presidential administration since that of the late Mr. McKinley by declaring, "Richard Nixon and his men were, for the first time in American politics since 1860, carrying on an ideological war." At another point he speaks of America's ethnic diversification in such exaggerated terms as to leave the impression that the United States is at one with the late Austro-Hungarian Empire. This is historical revisionism in sheep's clothing.

Yet, whereas some revisionists twist the record because of their ideological fevers or because their wives laugh at them for lingering at the bottom of the academic ladder, White revises the record because to him the record does not matter. What matters is sheer pomp and noisiness. Thanks to his amazing gusto for the art of Methodist ranter, he has succeeded in his quest. He has developed a kind of book whose bombast could waken the dead. It is a glory: "Middle America had been without a great leader for generations, and in Richard Nixon, it had elevated a man of talent and ability, a President so powerful that Richard Nixon alone had been able to destroy Richard Nixon. . . . The Nixon disaster has ushered in the new 94th Congress—overwhelmingly Democratic, refreshingly vigorous, more determined than any Congress since 1866 to curb Presidential authority. . . . The new Congress has astounded and delighted all observers by its first efforts to make the Congress responsible to the changing needs of a new generation of Americans. . . ." Ah, yes, the famed 94th Congress; and the delight, how we remember the delight; and the changing needs; and the new generation; and the noise— the goddam, incessant, mind-jangling noise. There will come a day when, the First Amendment notwithstanding, White's books will be banned in every hospital zone in the country. But for the 1970s, the decade of digitalis and meaninglessness, the books were powerful stuff.

Public Nuisances

POSTSCRIPT

The *New York Times*, July 14, 1978: "Representative John Brademas of Indiana . . . accepted $2,950 in $50 bills from a foreign national at a time when he was involved in drafting legislation to prohibit such contributions, the House ethics committee reported today. . . . the committee also criticized Representative Thomas P. O'Neill, Jr., the House Speaker, for permitting himself to be the guest of honor at two Washington parties given by Tongsun Park. . . . Although the House committee filed formal complaints yesterday against four Congressmen . . . the committee took no official action against Mr. Brademas [or] Mr. O'Neill."

Theodore White, *Breach of Faith*, 1975: "To be a man of the House is to be part of a special circle of loyalties . . . as is John Brademas of Indiana, or 'Tip' O'Neill of Massachusetts. To be a man of the House requires not only that one understand its parliamentary trickeries but also that one love the House as an institution."

Mr. White improves with age!

5

Gore Vidal:
Fabulist Major

HOW ABUNDANT with curiosities is this land we call America, this Graeco-Roman tradition that eventuated in a melting pot. Our greatest author lives not here but in far-off Italy, as does our greatest literary critic, our greatest essayist, and one who but for his devotion to literature might have been the greatest leader of a democratic people since Lincoln. Who are these expatriates? They are one and the same. They are Gore Vidal himself alone. Mr. Vidal, the author of *Williwaw* and so many other memorable masterworks, lives in Ravello, south of Naples, where, as he says, "I do nothing but think about my country. The United States is my theme and all that dwell in it." I put this down as the purest act of patriotism since Jimmy Carter forsook the plow.

From a spectacular Romanesque villa commanding a cliff hundreds of feet above the Mediterranean Sea, Mr. Vidal looks ever westward, and with garlic fumes to his back, sedulously analyzes "the last empire on earth," capitalism run amok, and the horror of the "heterosexual dictatorship" that so oppresses the libidinous elf squirming within each and every American. It is an enormous undertaking. Yet the villa, built in 1927 by Countess Szechenyi, the daughter of Lord Grimthorpe, is spacious, serene, and secure, an ideal laboratory for Mr. Vidal's valuable cerebrations. The happy result has been a relentless stream of penetrating disquisitions, generally appearing in the *New York Review of Books*, but occasionally turning up in more abstruse journals like *Marxist Perspectives*. Of course, some of The Novels have been written in Ravello, and it is there that Mr. Vidal prepares the lectures that he gives during his annual invasion of the American Chautauqua circuit. His appearances on college campuses have been the high point in many a young student's educational development.

By his own admission Vidal is "a propagandist, a proselytizer, and a teacher." His earlier, less complicated writing made him a fortune of sorts, but today he is almost wholly devoted to writing literature for the ages and to apprising the world of the doom that awaits it if America does not follow a more enlightened course. Energetically he propagates his message of reason, progress, radical reform, and an end to the infernal doings of the Rockefellers. Few among the intelligentsia have been more selfless and single-minded. When the revolution finally comes one hopes that Mr. Vidal will be around to enjoy it. He deserves a time of dawn rather than an era of gloom. On the other hand, one has to hope that the revolution does not arrive in Italy before coming to America. It would be a highly vexatious disruption of Mr. Vidal's work were Comrade Berlinguer to expropriate his villa—a villa that has been an inspiration to a rising generation of radical thinkers in America. Championing radical reform here is difficult enough, and we intellectuals found great solace in the November/December 1974 issue of *Architectural Digest: The*

Connoisseur's Magazine of Fine Interior Design. There our brother's villa, named "La Rondinaia," was featured.

"It's heaven," Howard Austen has observed, "except for the phones and the servants. You get a couple, and either the woman is crazy or the man's a drunk . . . or both." Howard has been Gore's constant companion since 1950. "And the gardener, I'd rather not talk about *him*," Howard fumed. These judgments are recorded in a rare interview granted by the fellows to *Vogue* magazine in the early seventies. Admittedly, *Vogue* is not known to have a very intellectual readership, but then if one is truly serious about socialism and the heterosexual dictatorship one will carry the struggle to all parts. After all, even Hannah Arendt had to buy an occasional evening gown. And only Yahweh knows; some rainy afternoon not yet arrived a middle-aged Patty Hearst might just thumb through an ancient copy of *Vogue* and *ooooh* the old flame could rekindle, the *Internationale* could strike up anew, and the American establishment might again be staggered.

These are the kinds of calculations Gore and Howard must make, as the pasta boils in the kitchen and the gardener flummoxes in the sunshine amid "La Rondinaia's" six acres of lemon trees and flowers. I have followed Gore's work for years, and I like to think of him as a Frantz Fanon for upper Park Avenue; could it be that Howard is his Ché Guevara? The relationship has been a long one, and I cannot but believe that it has been full of high purpose. *Vogue* reports that "They are just good friends, nothing else now." And Howard allows as how "We each have our own friends, and we each respect what the other does." But precisely what does Howard do, and what has he been doing since 1950? There is mystery here. Gore fires off salvos at the Rockefeller conspiracy, lectures, and improves us with The Novels; but what is Howard's role? *Vogue* notifies us that his spinach soup and lemon chiffon pie are universally admired, but I have heard nothing of them. Just lolling around Gore's villa, making pies, and enduring the gardener—is the thing possible? Conceivably Howard, whose markedly boyish facade conceals a man of middle years, is Gore's contact with the Baader-Meinhof gang. Perhaps he clandestinely bankrolls a Puerto Rican bomb emporium or a liberation cabal as yet unactivated. Could he be in the pay of Arab idealists? A friend and advisor to Carlos (Fats) Martinez, the international terrorist? From his badinage in *Vogue* it is apparent he is a smooth operator. Yet maybe his association with Gore is entirely on the up and up. Gore could use a Boswell, and Howard assuredly understands the author's spiritual and intellectual depths: "He's crazy about peas, and he'll kill for baby potatoes and asparagus," Howard has declared authoritatively. This man is no fool. Whatever his role on this orb, my guess is that when he passes on to glory some lucky relative will be made heir to a vast collection of hitherto unknown watercolors full of dark meaning, poems that will inflame you, works of beauty. Gore could not exist without the company of deep thinkers.

Who is this jackanapes? Christened Eugene Luther Vidal, Jr.—he is now known simply as Gore Vidal (vē däl′) to his customers, and it is a rare Americano who has not at one time or another been his customer. He has written novels, mysteries, Hollywood and TV screenplays, book reviews, essays, and poems. Furthermore he has appeared on television more often than Idi Amin. It was through the medium of television that he essayed to rid America of William F. Buckley, Jr., a man who quite definitely, albeit curiously, unhinges Gore. The noble effort began in January 1962, on a national TV talk show during which Gore, then as now a confirmed pagan, charged that Buckley had attacked no less an eminence than the Pope. The Pope, at least in the early sixties, was in espe-

Gore Vidal

cially good odor with TV junkies, and Gore found the battle joined. Full of duty and courage, he set out to elucidate the frightening dimensions of right-wingery then being resurrected by this Buckley. That is to say, he turned up every few nights before the country's insomniacs to malign Buckley, his family, and his friends. The war ended sadly for Gore when he appeared face to face with the fabled debater on New York's "Les Crane Show"; as one reviewer characterized it, Gore had his flesh nibbled off by "a fair-haired barracuda named William Buckley, Jr."

Gore was, in time, to suffer greater ignominies at Buckley's hands. Nevertheless he pursued him doggedly and somewhat rabidly, much the way he was then pursuing Norman Mailer.

Public Nuisances

Gore's struggles continue, and the beatings inflicted on him have been fearful. Buckley merely outwits him, while Mailer actually does him violence, often pausing during cocktail parties to paste him a good one. Before a TV appearance back in the early seventies, Mailer spotted him backstage, butted him smartly in the coco, and sent him spinning onto the stage looking queasy and confounded.

This passion for altercation and punishment has marked Gore's entire career. Sometimes he carries the day: thrown in with some fundamentalist Christian or some dull-witted congressman, he bludgeons his prey as the audience marvels, if not at his compassion, then at his urbanity and intelligence. But thrown in with someone who knows what's what, he either falls sullen and silent or makes the fur fly and retreats furless. It is during these butcherings that Gore gives himself away, betraying the source of all his assorted varieties of moonshine. Poor Gore is emotionally frozen into early adolescence and a particularly turbulent adolescence at that. He is boyish. He is girlish. And when under pressure he is feverish. During his concession speech after the "Les Crane Show" a woebegone Gore admitted that with Buckley he had become "emotionally involved." Buckley must have had some uneasy moments digesting that revelation, and Howard Austen must have been in despair.

Yet if one considers the whole of Gore's public life, all those years of preposterous pronunciamentoes and fantastic poses, one gets the impression that he has become "emotionally involved" more often than might be expected of a middle-aged writer. Many of the things he claims to believe are purely idiotic: ". . . we [Americans] never talk about anything very important. . . . We don't say that 4 percent of the people own the country . . ."; "one of every five people in the U. S. is mentally disturbed . . ."; and the first and second world wars destroyed the old European empires, and created ours. In 1945 we were the world's greatest power. . . . Unfortunately those industries that had become rich during the war *combined* with the military [creating] a vast military establishment.

Officially this was to protect us from the evil Commies. Actually it was to continue pumping federal money into companies like Boeing and Lockheed and keep the Pentagon full of generals and admirals while filling the pork barrels of congressmen. . . .

Nobody in particular was to blame. It just happened. To justify our having become a garrison state, gallant Harry Truman set about deliberately alarming the American people. The Soviet was dangerous. We must have new and expensive weapon systems. To defend the free world. The cold war began. The irony is that the Soviet was not dangerous to us *at that time.* *

History made intelligible for mental defectives.

Other testimonials reveal an intellect that is itself not all that powerful: "The true end of a democratic society is economic equality; that's an idea whose time has not come. But it's implicit in the idea of democracy, and when our system collapses and gas and food and everything has to be rationed we'll realize that was our goal anyway"; or "Sirhan grew up in Pasadena, a center of the John Birch Society, a center of radical right reactionaries, a despicable blot on this earth. The people of Pasadena are well off. They hate the Jews, they hate the Negroes, the poor, the foreign. I find these to be really terrible people. Sirhan grew up in this atmosphere and I do not doubt that he heard many anti-Kennedy speeches. He simply accepted the way people in Pasadena think. He decided that Bobby Kennedy was evil and he killed him. . . ." Surely a truly second-rate mind could do better than this.

His lack of, shall we say, fixity is legendary. Vidal, August

* From Gore Vidal, "The State of the Union," in *Matters of Fact and Fiction: Essays 1973–1976.* Copyright © 1977 by Random House. Reprinted by permission. "The State of the Union" originally appeared in Esquire, May 1975.

25, 1968: "Well, it is the greater wisdom, finally to trust the people." Vidal, spring 1963: "One must never underestimate the collective ignorance of that informed electorate for whom Thomas Jefferson had such high hopes." Vidal, November 1968: "I have always felt that we must never underestimate the essential bigotry of the white majority in the United States." Vidal, December 1974: "Most Americans are liars or crooks if they can get away with it." On August 5, 1968, he informed a national television audience that thirty million Americans were living in poverty; two nights later the figure inexplicably dropped to twenty-two million; but then in the *New York Review of Books* he spoke of "forty million poor." It was about this that he solemnly declared: "For myself, should the war continue after the 1968 election, a change in nationality will be the only moral response." The change, of course, was never consummated, but it would have been a swell show had Gore become a Cambodian. Think of the frantic calls that would have gone out from some fashionable neighborhood in Phnom Penh during that tragic April in 1975, desperate calls to the "last empire on earth."

That his political mentor was Eleanor Roosevelt has long been known. He speaks of her often and fondly: the time he caught her arranging flowers in a toilet bowl, the "thorny Puritan American conscience" (which he admires!), the "stoic serenity," the "conscience to the world." To Gore she was an American Socrates, and he will be eulogizing her for years to come. When he stifles his polemical oratory long enough to lay forth a political program it becomes clear that his is the most authentic projection of the mind of Eleanor now operating in America. National health care is a must, and Gore will not rest until America has an educational system and a mass-transit system the equal of those serving some unnamed Euro-

pean paradise. As visionaries go Gore is of the magnitude of
the League of Women Voters, circa 1960.

Gore is the grandson of Senator Thomas Gore, an Oklahoma populist whose memory time has somehow obscured for
all save Gore, who makes the cranky old gasbag out to be this
century's John C. Calhoun. Next to sex, politics appears to be
Gore's favorite realm of fantasy, and it is apparent that in his
political fantasies Gore has often seen himself as a statesman of
moment. In 1960 the fantasy took life; he ran for Congress in
New York's 29th district. Now all the profligacy of his youth
was decorously shoved behind the arras. His homosexual novels, his carousals with Tennessee Williams and other such
louts, his mawkish interludes with Anaïs Nin, his proud pil-
grimage to André Gide, his Hollywood years. In pursuit of the
congressman's gaud no indignity was beneath him. He even
composed a slogan, "You'll Get More With Gore." Twenty-
five thousand votes were the thin membrane between defeat
and a rebirth of the American Republic. Still, the political
fantasy lingers. In 1974 he declared to a startled interviewer
that he had moved to Italy in the early 1960s "because I was
giving up practical politics and trying to avoid being drafted to
run again for the House in '64. I knew that if I went on living
up the Hudson, I'd be a full-time politician and never write
again." And so Gore returned to his Art.

How fine are The Novels? The trashiness of American literary tastes is one of Gore's favorite and most persuasive proposi-
tions. That his popularity with American readers has not diminished his superlative estimate of his own literary merit is
another colossal example of his talent for self-deception. Gore
is of course a frequent author of best sellers; nonetheless he
places himself "at the top of the heap," while disparaging
Faulkner, Hemingway, and practically all his more gifted fore-

Public Nuisances

bears. Precisely whom he does admire is not easy to establish, his penchant for contradiction being as active in literary judgments as in political asseverations. In the fall 1974 issue of the *Paris Review* he notified the literary world that "There's only one living writer in English that I entirely admire . . . William Golding." In November 1974, when Gore placed himself "at the top of the heap," he did not even include Golding in the heap. We know that he does admire the late critic Edmund Wilson, because he has compared Wilson to himself. Still almost no other writer is ever allowed such unqualified praise.

Actually, Gore's life as a novelist is only a little less illusory than his life as a politician. True, he actually does write novels, but no critic worth his salt has ever taken one of them seriously. His first novels, full of savorless prose and cardboard characters, were unappealing imitations of the works of his superiors. In 1954 he retired from *belles lettres* to write for TV and the movies. When he finally returned to the novel he brought with him a professionalism that can only be learned in the clever company of Hollywood hacks. His recent books all show the Hollywood touch, with their casts of morons, their faked emotions, their utterly idiotic portrayals of reality. They are all best sellers and all provide irrefutable support for his criticism of the best-seller list.

Whether Gore is really pleased with his performance I have no way of knowing, but his success has not been without heartache. In 1975 the rascal Buckley struck out at him. While skiing in Switzerland Buckley threw off a novel of his own, *Saving the Queen*. By 1976 the book had made the bestseller list, right up there with Gore's *1876*. This must have been a grim time back in Ravello. There they were together, the Great Novelist and William F. Buckley, Jr. I have read all Gore's ambitious works plus *Saving the Queen*; alas, the amateur Buckley with his first thrust came close to the top of the heap. In 1978 Buckley struck again, this time just as Gore came out with a repellent little book called *Kalki*. Buckley's was *Stained Glass*, a really creditable novel that leapt to the top of the best-seller list even as Gore clawed madly to hold on to its lowest rungs. For a creature of Gore's cosmopolitan tastes, a pummelling at the hands of Norman Mailer undoubtedly has its satisfactions. But to have had one's novels surpassed by William F. Buckley, Jr., must have been an experience of unredeemed grief.

Through the years Gore has learned to write fluent and amusing essays, but here too he lives a life of fantasy. He has come to think himself an intellectual of the first water. He knows the arcana of the ancients, world literature, the quiddities of enlightened policy. So far as I am able to ascertain, it is all humbug. Reflecting on his first novel, he once admitted "I was . . . easily the cleverest young fox ever to know how to disguise his ignorance and make a virtue of his limitations." The fox slinks on.

Gore's portrayal of homosexuality's place in the ancient world is either ignorant or dissembling. His sense of history is erratic. At times he sounds like the brightest graduate student ever to take a Masters of Education degree at Cleveland State University. Other times he is either being a tease or making heavy weather of it with information that any moderately intelligent college freshman attains after an elementary course. He has no serious ideas about history, though he has written several historical novels. In fact it is doubtful that he has any serious ideas at all. He is a man of turbulent passions and irrational prejudices.

Gore makes a very big thing out of the derisible character of the middle-class American burgher, who in Gore's composite has large elements of George Babbitt and George Wallace along with just a vague suggestion of Nelson Rockefeller. Doubtless a sizable minority of Americans are just as bigoted, intolerant, smug, and stupid as Gore insists; but what is really riveting is the frequency of his own lapses into these deficiencies. The creed of many of his villains, their traits, and the nature of his complaint against Mailer betray a congeries of prejudices which looks like nothing so much as anti-Semitism. Violence and cruelty inhere through many of his novels, notably *Myra Breckenridge*, and his humanitarian protest that Mailer and Henry Miller celebrate violence and "hatred of women" is the campaign oratory of a popinjay fighting to maintain his status as TV sage.

Whether Mailer is more taken up with violence than Vidal I leave to other minds, but certainly to speak of Miller in this way is to mislead. As a novelist Miller towers over Vidal. With intellectual courage and emotional sincerity, Miller wrote some of the finest American novels of the century. His is, in the words of George Orwell, ". . . a friendly American voice, with no humbug in it. . . ." In other words he is the precise opposite of Vidal. It is fitting that Miller should live his last days in a quiet California neighborhood, confident in his authorship of many fine books and utterly remote from the fantasies of Ravello.

Yet back in the villa the great work continues. Novels are sketched, bad books reviewed, and more and more conspiracy theories of American life are hatched. Through the years Gore's conspiracy theories have grown increasingly outlandish, as they approximate ever more closely those of the lunatic right. It is a delicious symmetry.

On summer nights the villa fills with the most renowned left-wing intellectuals of the West. In the soft light of the great vaulted living room sit Claire Bloom, Mick and Bianca Jagger, Princess Margaret, and the scholarly Newmans, Joanne and

Paul. The talk turns to health care, and Gore laments that our system compares unfavorably with the barber shops of the last Persian empire, one of the few cultures he still admires (he finds it "subtle"). Princess Margaret speaks of Chile, and Howard Austen turns the discussion to Gore's shoes: "He had three pairs made in London twenty years ago. They're falling apart. . . . What *can* you do with him?" Paul Newman launches into a discourse on a new econometric model that might bring the whole world up to the nutritional standards of Malibu Beach. And Howard opines that Gore's diets are "dangerous." He goes "from gluttony to starvation. It's voluptuous and maybe autosexually satisfying, and his diets might be a sort of rebirth, but I think they're too traumatic for the body." Far into the Mediterranean night the colloquy goes. Let the Rockefellers, the generals, and the other rulers of the heterosexual dictatorship work their wicked wills. In Ravello, the flame of idealism still burns, and if Gore has his way, by God, it will become a general conflagration.

6

Robert Coover: Fabulist Minor

ROBERT LOWELL COOVER is a writer who, for a man of middle years, invests an unusual number of his waking hours thinking about underpants. And so very intellectual are the thoughts underpants inspire in him that many prominent universities pay him hard cash to take up residence and think some more. Life with the profs and the collegians apparently appeals to Coover, for he has spent most of his adult years in such challenging environs as Wisconsin State University, in dynamic Superior, Wisconsin, where he served as writer in residence and, if I know my fish, kept the local juvenile authorities hopping.

Coover is one of those academically inclined novelists who roost on or near college campuses, attentively gathering preposterous theories from crank pedants and transforming them into literature . . . from fiction to fiction, the life cycle of an ideologue's truths. All the trendy moonshine born of the bogus learning of sociologists, psychologists, and other certified *poseurs* turns up in Coover. His is a busy afflatus, and never could elucidating the significance of American undergarments satisfy his genius. He has dared to peer beyond, and as the Coover *oeuvre* unfolds we see him assiduously probing the real meanings of armpits, halitosis, nocturnal emissions, and every imaginable aspect of the toilet stool—matters too long shunned by the nation's less worldly, less percipient writers. Here, in areas once thought to be the special preserve of hospital orderlies and washroom attendants, Coover finds occasion for historical, philosophical, political, and even theological statement. Thus Coover's audience is limited. His complicated masterpieces are for progressives of a decidedly academic inclination: who but the willing victims of faculty meetings and departmental cocktail parties would endure his message that human existence is bizarre, ghastly, and absurd? Not only is such a thesis girlishly melodramatic, it is unoriginal. Not surprisingly, Coover is one of the few young American writers in whose work Gore Vidal has found anything creditable.

Yet Coover spouts his stuff bravely in books, in plays, and at places like Bard College and Washington University in St. Louis, Missouri, where he has reigned as brooder in residence. Coover is—as Joseph Epstein once noted—an ardent member of the adversary culture, and so his absorption with what admirers call "the cosmic questions" has about it a ludicrous predictability and an invincible ignorance. Once boomed as an intelligently critical stance toward western bourgeois society, the adversary culture has in recent decades settled into a smug orthodoxy celebrating values antithetical to bourgeois society, namely: unreason, intolerance, coercion, and cultural primitivism, plus anti-anti-Communism and anti-Americanism. This is the stance that so idiotizes modern novelists that many of them are capable of believing, along with Coover and E. L. Doctorow, almost any elaborate conspiracy not solely confected by the John Birch Society.

All of the adversary culture's advanced values inhere throughout Coover's 1977 book, *The Public Burning*, an unspeakably dreary 534-page scow of a novel that shudders along propelled by at least three inverted insights: (a) the Rosenbergs were innocent of espionage and only guilty of being quite the nicest Americans since Sacco and Vanzetti; (b) the villainous United States government framed these two patriots as "expiatory victims of the cold war"; and (c) Russian Communism in the early 1950s was harmless if indeed it even existed. Coover depicts Russian Communism as "The Phantom," a gimcrack term evincing his artistic indebtedness to comic books and TV.

As with so many of the modern academic novelists Coover prides himself not only as an investigator of "cosmic questions," but also as a theoretician of the novel. "[W]hen something hits us strong enough, it means it's something real," he is quoted as having said in *Critique* magazine, and in *The Public Burning* he wallops his readers with one colossal reality after another. Thought-provoking is the scene in which Vice-President Richard Nixon secretes himself in Ethel Rosenberg's cell for an amorous tryst shortly before 2,000 volts of electricity make her a saint. Then, too, there is the dramatic moment when members of the Supreme Court struggle through lush mounds of elephant droppings en route to the Times Square execution of Ethel and her mate. And finally, in a scene that bids fair to become one of the most pondered passages in American literature, Uncle Sam anoints Richard Nixon for the presidency by sodomizing him. Some two thousand words are devoted to this metaphysical exchange, and from the finely detailed sketch of the impaled Nixon one can only conclude

68

that the scene is the product of years of first-hand research by the author.

How these scenes of "something real" affect other readers I cannot say; but they had a fearsome impact on me, causing great freshets of perspiration to run from my brow and putting an unexpected curl in my hair. For me Times Square will never seem quite the same. Henceforth I shall furtively sniff every passing breeze for one last whiff of the noble Ethel, hoping always not to mistake her for that elephant manure. The image of Nixon amorously fondling the Marxist-Leninist Beelzebub banished forever the lingering admiration I held for our 37th president. I am transformed. This is art.

But it is the art of a bygone era. Today the profit margins are down for 1960s barbarism and for that easy nihilism so frequently manufactured by holders of Guggenheim Fellowships and Rockefeller Foundation grants. It was after a period of huge anticipation in the literary world that in 1977 *The Public Burning* slid down the ways, steamed out into the channel, and sank. The faithful did everything they could to salvage it. Professor Thomas R. Edwards hollered from the *New York Times Book Review* that the wreck was actually "an extraordinary act of moral passion." In the *New Republic* a genuine teacher of contemporary fiction from the University of Cincinnati hailed it as "a major achievement of conscience and imagination." But the musky fragrance of moral passion, conscience, and imagination could not arouse the old clientele. After Solzhenitsyn and Cambodia, America-loathing and anti-Communist-loathing are not such alluring literary props. Somewhere at this very hour Coover doubtless is dreaming up new philosophical metaphors—why not a U.S. senator undone by bushy nose hair? What of a Supreme Court justice with incurable flatulence?—but he dreams in obscurity.

Public Nuisances

Whole armies of hacks would have to be exterminated before readers would turn to him.

The Public Burning was momentous in its failure. Technically flawed, intellectually unserviceable, stupefyingly boring, it was prodigiously worthy of being hailed as the 1960s' last gasp. Coover will, of course, go on writing his incivistic idiocy, and his college constituency will remain. But it will not grow; the era is over. New lunatic enthusiasms will replace it, but I doubt Coover will be nimble enough to adapt to them. He lacks the talent of a Vidal. So long dogberry.

7

Bob Dylan:
Prophet to a Generation

OF BOB DYLAN'S LYRICS it has been said that they were filigreed with "metaphysical subtleties" and "surrealistic epigrams." Of the composer himself, it has been laid down that he was "a reluctant Eumenides," the "conscience" and "oracle" of his generation. Can you see it: Bob Dylan, the oracle of *our* generation, whispering into the ear of Donald Segretti; Dylan, the public conscience of Charles Manson!

Such nauseating folderol devoted to a hack and a charlatan was not minted in the far-off, balmy 1960s. Not this stuff. It was uttered in the 1970s after more than a decade of abuse from the Schubert of Hibbing, Minnesota. And it was issued not solely from those vacuous cheerleaders of pop who rephrase press releases at mass magazines. There were also very fastidious scholars who extolled the wart Dylan: for instance, an erstwhile Columbia prof now terrifying students of English at Queen's College with revelations such as: "like only a few of the most interesting artists, his [Dylan's] shifts reveal those of the age, as if the Hegelian *Zeitgeist* had for a space of time come to rest on his shoulders." The wisdom is that of Professor Doctor Morris Dickstein, and it appeared in his incomparable *Gates of Eden*, a book. Possibly the learned doctor is practicing irony.

During the late 1960s and early 1970s one could always rely on pop music critics for comic relief, and the more educated the critic claimed to be the more hilarious his remarks. How well I remember Dr. Richard Poirier, Distinguished Professor of English at Rutgers University, and his fabulous yawp to the Beatles. It was sheer Keystone Kops, made all the more amusing by the fact that this lovable Malvolio had actually written *The Comic Sense of Henry James*. According to Dr. Poirier, ". . . sometimes the Beatles are like Monteverdi and sometimes their songs are even better than Schumann's. . . . The Beatles exist not merely as a phenomenon of entertainment but as a force of historical consequence." These thoughts were uttered in *Partisan Review*, and made available to the general public in a book that became very popular amongst the profs.

The only thing more amusing than a sap commenting on Bob Dylan is Dylan commenting on himself. His concerts were populous with intellectualoids, and intellectualoids have a flare for, as they say, verbalizing. His 1974 Chicago concert contained such American originals as: a twenty-eight-year-old teacher who held forth at *two* Montessori schools by day and the Chicago Art Institute by night; a vegetarian from the Department of Transportation; a youthful part-time builder of geodesic domes; and a seventeen-year-old artist judged by her parents and herself to be a prodigy so gifted that the whole family gladly journeyed from Milwaukee to set up an artistic synergism between her, howling in the audience, and him, whining on stage.

Her father, a middle-aged creative-type from the advertising industry, and his thoughtful wife sounded like this: Father: "You couldn't classify my wife and myself as rock freaks, but Dylan isn't Tin Pan Alley stuff. The difference is his message." Mother: "Our generation didn't accept the protest of the 1960s at the time. Dylan was disgusted with parts of society as we all were, but he put it into music. He helped to bring a lot of my generation around to realizing some of the falseness in our society."

Yokels like this will always make our trip from *hee* to *haw* an effortless one. We should be grateful for every word they utter. According to the begetter of domes, Dylan was "not a god; more like a genius." The seventeen-year-old Goya was more specific: "He's the most important musician who ever lived— more important than Ludwig van Beethoven." And the twenty-eight-year-old pedagogue, ah, he is modernity itself; and, as Madame Montessori is no longer with us to object, I shall quote him in his entirety: "I've been listening to Dylan since 1966. I've been really heavily into him for about the last five years. *Nashville Skyline* [one of Dylan's country albums] is okay, but it's not the Dylan I needed when I listened to him back then. I mean, I was going through some personal changes, and his crazy imagery was a good escape for me."

Was there ever any truth in these breathless effusions? Frankly, I have some doubts. Perhaps Dylan had Beethoven's manners. From his public statements it is obvious he shared Beethoven's humility. And it is clear he equalled the German cad's integrity, but then there is the matter of art. Did "The Times They Are A-Changin' " match the complexity of the Great Fugue? I shake my head, but perhaps complexity is not the soul of the issue, and possibly we would follow a more fruitful line of inquiry were we to ask whether or no these two compositions share the same timeless beauty. Does "The Times They Are A-Changin' " transport the spirit? Will it do so tomorrow? Our part-time builder of geodesic domes, will his progeny find Dylan's work as lovely as did pa? Dubiety steals in, but for the nonce let us leave these ponderosities and behold the master himself. Bob Dylan—minstrel, metaphysician, millionaire.

The most eloquent evidence of his intellect still resides in a remarkable statement he made in 1974 to an apparently enthralled reporter from *Newsweek,* a journal that has come to be a kind of intellectualoids' delicatessen. According to Mr. Dylan: "Saturn has been an obstacle in my planetary system. It's been there for the last few ages and just removed itself from my system. I feel free and unburdened." College sophomores should bear this in mind the next time Dr. Dickstein lectures them on Dylan's genius. And when they are abused with that claptrap about his being the conscience of an era, they should remember how Dylan squirmed through this question relating to the handsome profits his art fetches him: "I'd be doing what I'm doing if I was a millionaire or not, whether I was getting paid for it or not. In the sixties there was a certain bunch of us who came through the wars. There was a lot of death during that time. The sixties were filled with it. It has helped me to grow up. The seventies are more realistic, but the sixties exposed the roots of that realism." Some days later, still caught up on the same subject—namely himself—Dylan informed *Time:* "All this publicity, sometimes I think they're talking about somebody else. I take it as it comes, but I'm not certain its beneficial to my life." It is not without reason that Dylan has chosen to avoid public interviews—a few more embarrassments of that magnitude and Woody Allen will be making movies about this lyrical conscience.

Still, despite the pedestrian quality of the man's mind and my unscotchable suspicion that his musical gifts are on a par with those of, say, the late Glenn Miller, Dylan does possess a talent for suckering the gulls. In a word he has charisma, that curious narcotic that reduces the most gnarled cynic to the gentleness of a cooing babe even in this glorious era of compulsory impiety. How he acquired this mysterious effluvium I know not, but the fact remains that he sparkles with the stuff. The ring left by him in his heart-shaped bathtub would doubtless contain enough of it to make Edmund Muskie president for life.

With charisma a man has a huge and unfair advantage over his fellows. No socialist state will ever be up to snuff until it is prohibited. The man who has it can fix his eyes on an audience, and its members hear a faint trumpet sounding on a far-off horizon. He nods his head or waves an arm, and they see Caesar. When he sighs they think of Goethe. When he groans they hear Brahms. And his utterances, no matter how platitudinous or paralogistic, always contain enough ellipses to allow his listeners to assume that they are in the presence of a man to conjure with. Yet, through all his theatrics, the spellbinder, I suspect, really has his mind on matters far remote from his audience. Charisma is that solemnity of countenance that deludes an audience into thinking it is in the presence of a truly stupendous spirit even when all the great man is thinking about is how he longs to slip into a dry pair of socks. I have watched charisma illuminate some of the political greats of our era. I submit that it is a major ingredient in the success of large numbers of America's pop idols. Dylan surely has it. What separates him from Rod McKuen is a fleeting encounter with Arthur Rimbaud and E. E. Cummings, an apprenticeship in Greenwich Village, and little more.

Sometime in the 1960s a handful of profs, rigidly trained in the lore of academe, abandoned themselves to the delights of popular culture; and on the morning after they felt guilt-ridden by their fall. How could they tell their colleagues that they had been fetched by a tune on the AM band of their foreign car? How could they admit to having listened to the AM band? From sheer vanity they justified their discovery by turning out pedagogical tracts elevating pop culture to levels of profundity and complexity hitherto beyond the reach of any creative genius save the very greatest. Some of the profs, like Herbert Gans, even claimed their discoveries to be an indication of their superior democratic spirit. At any rate, they were all engaged in a great fraud against the *demos*. Denying the diverting banality of pop culture while investing it with highfalutin values is no testimonial to the plain folk. Of course the *demós* never swallowed this rubbish, but the profs' bulls were just what the intellectualoids desired, and soon some of the profs were renowned and prospering. The apotheosis of Dylan proved once again the enormous lust of the demieducated *poseur* for delusion.

As for the genius himself, though it took years, an accurate estimate of the man finally appeared in 1977, thanks to the more independently minded critics of Moscow's *Literaturnaya Gazeta*. According to the comrades and despite Dylan's mountain of protest songs, he tested out to be merely another grasping capitalist. That was their judgment. Such news must have come as a shock to the poet at his Malibu retreat, and it will surely finish him off with Dr. Dickstein and Dr. Poirier. But imagine the celebration over at the national headquarters of the Chamber of Commerce! Bob Dylan—his lawyers, his accountants, and his PR hack—finally they are out of the closet!

PART

II

THE PUBLIC NUISANCE AS LOUSE

8

The Louse Today

As WITH SO MANY THINGS, there is in art a synergism, a collaboration between the artist and the fragrances,
the wails, the rhythms of his environment. The artist, if he is
worth his salt, has one ear cocked toward the chatter and
bustle of the living. He inhales life in voluptuous gulps. What
he exhales, naturally enough, he sells. All this is common
knowledge amongst cultivated readers and demands no further
commentary. Yet before discussing the nuisances of the next
few chapters it might be worthwhile to meditate on the odd
collaboration that today goes on between the educated classes
and the criminal element. The thing is preposterous, but it
goes on all the time. How many famed writers have lived a life
unblemished by championing at least one louse? How many
selections for the Book-of-the-Month Club celebrate the adventures of rogues and the reasoning of lunatics?

As a matter of scholarly interest, there is in the works of
most writers a curious hankering for the louse element; it is a
hankering shared by their audiences. In *Beyond Good and Evil*
the late Mr. Friedrich Nietzsche put it just so when he ob-

Public Nuisances

served that writers "are in the habit of taking the side of criminals." He might have added that so are readers and, come to think of it, even nonreaders—a point tellingly demonstrated in John Millington Synge's *The Playboy of the Western World*. In that illuminating work a wretched youth walks into a strange Irish village, allows as how he has achieved patricide by means of a common household shovel, and becomes a figure of awe. In recent years the Black Panthers achieved as much, so did Charles Manson and his followers, so did Joan Little, and doubtless there will be others.

There is today a widespread enchantment with what is squalid and iniquitous. It inheres through all classes, but it seems to be especially rampant amongst the upper classes and the better educated, that is to say, amongst those least exposed to the unpleasantness of squalor and iniquity. One could see it all emerging earlier in the century when the *vox populi* glamorized swine like Dillinger and Capone, and when sage and amiable degenerates began wandering into the works of the O'Neills and the Hemingways. Often the art was genuine, and the insights edifying; but as year piled upon year the louse motif became more salient and its message more dubious.

During the 1930s Steinbeck often wrote as though a paisano wino, moonlighting as a thug, were a born philosopher. Deadbeats came off as founts of moral philosophy, and ladies of the night were so often likened to the Little Sisters of Charity that by the 1950s many college boys believed that the remuneration received by the ladies went directly to the local almshouse. Many tipped the girls handsomely, and doubtless there was always a gullible businessman inquiring as to whether or no his payments were tax deductible.

Perhaps our present fascination with the louse element is no more illogical or misconceived than in years past. But we are assuredly pursuing more wicked varieties of criminals, and the legends we confect about them have certainly increased in absurdity. Nowadays the plight of a forlorn prostitute or a foreign-born mugger moves the lit. set not at all. They conserve their creative energies for terrorists, sadistic pederasts, kidnappers, and other such desperadoes. These they portray as tortured, sensitive, creative souls—troubled geniuses and ideal companions for one's literary teas or for TV chatter shows. "Interesting" books are written about the heroic struggles of murderers. Mass murderers too are lamented and analyzed. If the trend continues I can well imagine the day when even the villainous Nixon will become the stuff of romantic literature, though I doubt that this particular breakthrough will come in our lifetimes. Yet look at the eminence achieved by John Dean. In our era all things are possible if only the deception is blatant enough.

I cite the above not out of any moral prissiness or philistinism, but rather because I find it all ironic and without sense. How peculiar that the very same Americanoes who have abandoned themselves to a dither of goody-goodyism on questions of social policy should simultaneously become fascinated with the doings of swindlers, butchers, and common rogues! How moronic that writers should romanticize these miscreants! My guess is that your average scoundrel is not in and of himself any more interesting than a male hairdresser or a chauffeur of semitrailers. Most have little to say that is not arrantly self-serving and stupid. In this they are even more obvious than the dozens of presidential candidates at large in America on almost any day of the year. Some have managed to mimic the flummeries of left-liberal enlightenment, a matter that ingratiates them to thousands of forward-lookers. So what? The editor of *Saturday Review* learned to do that years ago, and no one has ever attempted to make a cult figure out of him. Hardly anyone even knows his name.

The lives of most criminals are vulgar beyond belief. The literary set might romanticize them as heroic exceptions to the bourgeois sludge, but can you imagine a clod of tawdrier tastes than, say, Joey Gallo, the subject of innumerable columns, a book, and now a Hollywood movie? It took very little meditation to convince me that the consumer preferences of the late Dillinger were indistinguishable from those of millions of Babbitts, and my guess is that Huey Newton's tastes are much the same as those of Anita Bryant. What piquant thought has Charles Manson or Richard Speck ever placed in the public domain? The likes and utterances of the departed ladies of the Symbionese Liberation Army are at one with those of the thousands of not very bright sorority girls all over America. Well I remember the time National Public Radio solicited golden nuggets on the criminal code from Mr. Clifford Irving, the poor fish caught *flagrante delicto* peddling a bogus Howard Hughes autobiography, and better still I remember his reply. He sounded like a cut-rate version of William O. Douglas. Let me state it here and now: notwithstanding the celebrity and commiseration sloshed on them by the educated classes, I would be willing to bet the price of lunch with John Kenneth Galbraith that the louse element consumes more nauseating cologne, more double-knit rags, more nonce gadgetry, and hardly less sociological mumbo-jumbo than any other element in our society. Members of the lit. set reflexively hold their noses when Jerry Ford comes to mind, but I doubt there is an inhabitant of one penitentiary in the land whose tastes are any finer.

Now if the literati and their readers have rhapsodized on the louse element it has been left to the social scientists to marshal the statistics and the syllogisms. For years giddy social scientists have been earning tenure by actively promoting the thesis that scoundrels of the worst sort are moved to their viciousness by circumstances. Often their treatises wholly depart from the statistics and assume the nature of poetry: the thug is virtuous, the society vicious. Some thugs are portrayed as debonair fellows full of fun and charm. Others are nascent geniuses of surpassing creativity who in another world would dwarf the achievements of Shakespeare. By playing on the average man's natural fascination with the criminal these charlatans foist a vast fraud upon us all.

If truth be known, the average American criminal is much more the Rotarian than one might suspect. Today's felons are often go-getters who have discovered what James Q. Wilson and Ernest van den Haag have been telling us for years, to wit: crime pays. The statistics are clear. If one commits a felonious crime in America today one is almost 98 percent certain of avoiding the hoosegow. The crime rate from 1960 to 1970 went up 144 percent, yet fewer persons served prison terms in 1970 than in 1960. Fresher statistics are not available, but it is obvious that if the crime rate has declined it has not declined much, and if the conviction rate is up it is up only marginally. Today an incautious young mugger might be inconvenienced by some red tape, possibly even an appearance in court, but his experience will not differ markedly from the experience of a small businessman confronted by a local regulatory agency. In fact, the criminal's experience is often more comfortable, for there is always the possibility he may appear before one of those modern judges whose insight it is that criminals are afflicted by society's ills or "victimized," thus deserving compassion and therapy.

Mr. Ramsey Clark has stated his doubt that "we achieve one

conviction for every fifty serious crimes." Even Edward Kennedy has lamented that "crime does pay." It is time to face up to reality: crime is a profession for which one needs no advanced degree, no period of apprenticeship, and no special insurance. The hours are generally discretionary, and one is subject to no foreman or boss of any kind unless one becomes a Mafioso, or joins one or another of the terrorist organizations. The tax bite is the lowest of all professions, and the Occupational Safety and Health Administration makes no demands, nor does the Consumer Products Safety Commission, nor the Federal Trade Commission, nor any other governmental regulatory agency. Enterprising Americans are taking advantage of the opportunities this field affords. The crime rate soars, even during periods of high employment and affluence, even during recessions.

Crime is a field with vast opportunities for young men and women who really want to get ahead. There is no evidence that these criminals are significantly different from individuals in any other walk of life, a point convincingly made in van den Haag's book *Punishing Criminals*. So let us forget all of this tomfoolery about the romantic character of the criminal. Snicker at the pap about his repressed creativity and his other sophisticated qualities. Let us face up to the real injustice; the American criminal is one of the most profit-minded members of his community. He is a go-getter of the top chop, and that there is no place for him in the Chamber of Commerce is an atrocity. Never has a practicing criminal been made one of the Jaycees' "Ten Outstanding Young Men" of America. This is bigotry, pristine and unadorned.

In the next few chapters I have gathered some of my favorite rogues and scoundrels of recent years. One or two have committed really barbarous acts; but most are mere rascals. The response to them by the so-called educated of the land tells us much about our era's trashy and contradictory values. Not one of these louses ignited the proper sense of outrage, and some were even the cause of libertarian testimonials and sympathetic analyses. James Madison would laugh. Even Thomas Jefferson would scowl.

9

Larry Flynt: Up from the Fuzzy Toilet Seat Cover

HOW INSCRUTABLE are the ways of history! Whoever would have imagined that someday our nation's most gifted intellectuals would be beholden to a dirty-necked grammar school dropout, suddenly risen from grubby obscurity to become America's foremost pimp and merchandiser of marital aids? But facts are facts, and in the late 1970s such high minded adepts of *la vie intellectuelle* as Gay Talese and Jann Wenner became inflamed over the enormities then being visited upon poor Mr. Larry Flynt (pronounced Flint), the animating genius behind Leasure Time Products and *Hustler* magazine. Thanks to Mr. Flynt the consciences of *poseurs* like Talese could again secrete their volupt discharges of moral indignation. Mr. Flynt gave them a heroic cause, and they were thankful. Suddenly, they could experience first-hand *l'affaire Dreyfus*, the Sacco and Vanzetti trial, the McCarthy era, and other horrors too dispiriting to recount. All they had to do was to sign a petition comparing the lower-court conviction of an

American millionaire to the imprisonment, torture, and extermination of thousands of Soviet dissidents. They were glad to do it. Opportunities for heroism in post-Nixonian America come so infrequently.

Biographical material on Mr. Flynt will always be scanty despite the lust for public relations that arose in him in later years. Simply put, there is little to say about him that is interesting or, for that matter, even uninteresting. At the time he became a *cause célèbre* he was in his mid-thirties, was trafficking in some of life's seedier goods, and had just entered into holy wedlock with one Althea Leasure, a cutie whose photographs suggested that she had a proclivity for spilling food on herself. In less than a decade the profits from his enterprises—profits that would be judged unconscionable were they amassed in any other business—had made him very rich. Yet, notwithstanding his mounds of money, Mr. Flynt remained a hopelessly pathetic slob. To the very end his life-style found its most precise metaphorical illumination in that peculiar American furnishing, the fuzzy toilet seat cover. In quality of mind and manner he remained at one with the likes of Mr. James Earl Ray and Mr. Juan Corona, the convicted killer of twenty-five farm workers. Though in fairness to Mr. Flynt it should be noted that he was more the humanist and civil libertarian. To listen to his defenders he was even somewhat of an intellectual, but then who is not nowadays.

At his emergence into public life Mr. Flynt fancied himself somewhat of a liberal, and at times he would send off ratiocinations reminiscent of the Rev. William Sloane Coffin, Jr., at the height of the 1960s, e.g.: "Obscenity is like the concept of sin—it defies definition. . . . In a free society nobody should be a judge." Eagerly he took up dozens of popular left-wing conspiracy theories and he even believed that the gunman who nearly ended his life in 1978 was a CIA agent. On the other hand he was given to pinning American flags on his leisure suits, and he apparently felt the stirrings of civic duty: *Hustler* began editorializing against the smoking menace on pages that might otherwise have featured a pair of brass knuckles, a whip, or an anus. Quite possibly his public-spiritedness would have goaded him into crusades against prostatitis, venereal disease, and some of those unmentionable kinds of cancer that so frequently vex his cosmopolitan readership. But all was nugatory and a botch, for as Mr. Flynt barged forward it became apparent that he was a born loser. Next to him Arthur Bremer appeared suave, accomplished, and fated for great things. At a booming time when a host of sex barons were freely publishing all ilk of prurient and perverse treasures, poor Mr. Flynt got himself convicted of "pandering obscenity and engaging in organized crime." Soon he was wriggling furiously to avoid seven to twenty-five years in an Ohio slammer. His public-spirited ravings grew more boisterous. He became a kind of randy populist, and he underwent a torrid conversion under the supervision of Ruth Carter Stapleton. Yet despite the fact that Sister Ruth had given him a fearsome dunking in the Blood of the Lamb he was barred from the Washington, D. C., Conference of Religious Broadcasters. At the White House not even Hamilton Jordan would hobnob with him, and then the CIA struck. The sex tycoon was paralyzed from the hips down.

Now I, as a strict civil libertarian, was as grateful to Mr. Flynt for his troubles as was Mr. Talese—but for different reasons. Mr. Talese was grateful for the opportunity solemnly to explicate his idiotic insight into "the connection between the sexual and the political." I was grateful because Mr. Flynt gave Mr. Talese this opportunity. It is extremely useful to have the moral quacks of the land blatantly displaying their hollowness, for it gives serious civil libertarians a chance to identify each other and to reflect on the country's intellectual rot. In most countries there exist multitudes of citizens who are threats to freedom and to culture, but in our modern era it is not so easy to point them out. They no longer live in the nation's backwaters, but have moved to the cities, taken over many of our cultural institutions, and learned to palm off their quackery as progressive thought and liberal vision. They exploit decent values for their own gain. What they did with Flynt was characteristic. They took one worthy principle of freedom—freedom of the press—disfigured it, and exploited it for their short-term profits. If they continue unchallenged, there will come a time when there will be no freedom of expression nor much freedom of any other sort, for they will have degraded freedom and dizzied society into disregarding completely the claims of freedom.

The war for Flynt's rights was always a farce waged by vicarious civil libertarians. During it the stage was alive with a mob of plastic Darrows hollering for a plaster Dreiser. No knowledgeable observer doubted for a moment that Flynt's legal counsel would eventually spring him. Serious defenders of civil liberties laughed when the vicarious civil libertarians compared Flynt to Soviet dissidents. No serious defender of freedom would ever raise such a fundamentally unimportant matter as "sexual expression" to the level of political and intellectual freedom.

For the most part America's vicarious civil libertarians of the 1970s are the same meretricious celebrities who provide crises and good causes for the Republic's intellectualoids. Illustrative of their character is the fact that prominent among them during the Flynt affair was Mr. John Dean, Watergate's Mary Magdalen turned author. Think of it—an "author" whose best seller was ghost-written defending a "dissident" whose dissidence made him one of the wealthiest and freest publishers in the world! If there were a serious threat to civil liberties in America, you can be sure that this pack of impostors would be over at Elaine's or another of their toney Manhattan saloons, primly sipping aperitifs, quoting the late Paul Elmer More, and eagerly awaiting the opportunity to stride forth on the pages of the *New York Times* as principled advocates of chaste reading and uplift.

Nothing is more revealing about our vicarious civil libertarians than their biographies. How many defenders of Larry Flynt ever rushed out in the early 1960s to defend the Negro as he struggled in the Deep South for some of the most elemental civil liberties? And even more instructive, how many actually journeyed to the Deep South to stand with Negro civil-rights activists who were getting their heads kicked in during marches and voter drives? How many speak out against the treatment accorded citizens behind the Iron Curtain? How many have parted with their loose nickels and dimes to support these poor souls? Since 1974 Alexander Solzhenitsyn has spent nearly a million dollars on the cause of civil liberties in the Soviet Union. How much support has Mr. Talese sent?

A sorry reality of contemporary America is that those bogus civil libertarians who make the noisiest spectacle of themselves on issues of human liberty generally know little about liberty and care less. They are either opportunists, posturers, or ignoramuses. This is true not only in the asinine debate over the First Amendment but also in the hyperbole of civil rights. Those hinds who have monopolized the public discourse comparing their conditions as women or as homosexuals to the historic oppression of blacks are frauds, freeloading on the misery of the past and on the compensatory impulse of the present. It is a shameful thing; black civil-rights spokesmen who allow this kind of bombast to go unchallenged are a curious lot.

The Great Republic abounds with white people who rue the fact that years ago they did not spy the Negro civil-rights movement for the winner that it proved to be and who now will leap on almost any so-called social justice bandwagon so long as it costs them little, is fashionable, and has a reasonable chance of giving them the feeling they are acting heroically on behalf of a historic sure thing. This is true of most of the so-called women's liberationists and even truer of the so-called homosexual-rights advocates.

Whether inspired by guilt or opportunism these frauds have become the worst nuisances since the reformers of yesteryear commenced their wars against Demon Rum and licentiousness. Not content with the traditional quack causes, today's nuisances have excogitated new ones. Even now there is a movement to extend civil rights to animals and to trees. Yet the ardor of these impostors is selective and skewed by fashion. In the case of Flynt all other ideals were abjured in deference to what was called his freedom of expression. Not only was Flynt to be free to exploit his readers, scorn women, humiliate decent working-class people, publish arrantly racist material, and sell fraudulent goods, but apparently he was to be free of any unfavorable judgment whatsoever. His excesses were hardly ever mentioned by anyone save the heinous and probably Hitlerite Cincinnati prosecutors.

There is a wonderfully absurd double standard that flourishes in these farces. If General Motors ever made the claims for a Buick that *Hustler* made for a set of genitals, Ralph Nader would lead a mob on Detroit. Flynt's production line included sex aids that looked like the instruments of a medieval torture chamber, yet if the sleuths from the Federal Trade Commission ever entered a complaint, Talese and his colleagues would have been howling persecution and demanding that the agency get back to the noble work of expurgating mouthwash ads and Wonder Bread wrappers. In all the pother over Flynt, not once did I hear any of the vicarious civil libertarians ever mention that along with the infantile sex Flynt also published blatantly racist stuff like cartoons depicting grotesque Negroes crawling toward rat traps baited with watermelon. *Hustler* probably published more racist aspersions in its heyday than any comparable magazine in decades and got off scot-free. Apparently the vicarious civil libertarians did not deem it appropriate even to comment on such matters, it being understood that suspension of judgment is essential to free speech.

As the years fall away it is ever more obvious that a vast number of liberals are really not terribly serious about liberalism. Mr. Talese equates sexual freedom ("sexuality" in his highfalutin argot) with political freedom. Think of it, the freedom to vote, to assemble, to form political parties, and to speak out on political issues is all of a piece with the freedom to sell marital aids. To quote Mr. Talese, "Sexuality is not divorced from the politics of government. Its suppression is entwined with attempts to regulate human behavior through control of imagery." Imagine how that lunatic yawp would go over with Vladimir Bukovsky and the starving prisoners of the Gulag! Assuming Mr. Talese is serious, his problem is a colossal inability to discriminate, and it is ironic that just this inability is what many First Amendment zealots charge against the American people.

They claim that free citizens are not capable of discriminating between pornography and *Ulysses*. But those who cannot discriminate between the condition of Andrei Sakharov and that of Mr. Larry Flynt are dubious judges of the judiciousness of others. There is a continuum from the total ban of pornography to total license. I see no reason why communities cannot opt for a policy that fits in between these two extremes.

Intelligent people can distinguish pornography from art. The rights of the pornographer can be balanced against the rights of a community that judges pornography baneful. One can make pornography less accessible without banning it totally. The claim that by regulating pornography's availability America glissades down a slippery slope toward total censorship is pristine and exquisite balderdash. If for its own survival each freedom must be given absolute license, why are our vicarious civil libertarians not exercised over income tax laws or the regulation of commerce? By limiting some income are we not on a slippery slope toward banning all income, or by limiting access to booze are we not on a slippery slope toward prohibition? No doubt speed limits put us on a slippery slope toward eliminating motion. The absurdity of the slippery slope argument stands up and roars for attention when one considers that those who use it to preserve and protect pornography are the very statists who so often demand strict regulation of commerce, affirmative action, busing, and other such tyrannies. And the nitwittery about slippery slopes aside, how much intelligence does it take to see the inevitable conflict of different freedoms, for instance, freedom of speech and freedom to privacy? Obviously in any free society judgments must be made about the boundaries of potentially conflicting freedoms.

Ah, but I theorize; and meanwhile back in the real world a fellow human being has been stalked, persecuted, almost assassinated. His cause was unpopular and even dangerous, and so it fell to idealists like Gay Talese, John Dean, and the editor

Public Nuisances

of the august *Rolling Stone* to answer liberty's call. Full of purpose and Jeffersonian oratory they marshalled the forces of liberty on behalf of the embattled Mr. Flynt. No wonder Alexander Solzhenitsyn moved to America. It must be enormously reassuring to him to know that down in Manhattan these idealists are paying the price of freedom. Who says America has no heroes?

10

Elmer Wayne Henley:
The Sorrow of Young Elmer

IS IT POSSIBLE to mark down young Elmer Wayne Henley—the convicted murderer of twenty-seven Houston children—as a failure? I believe it is. He repeatedly committed an act of extraordinary savagery, an act that, if committed in an earlier age, would have merited him enduring notoriety. Yet today hardly anyone remembers. What is more, almost no one ever did acknowledge the one quality he had undoubtedly mastered: wickedness.

The luckless young Elmer faded from American awareness with the swiftness of a Richard Speck or a Richard Whitman. Scoundrels of yesteryear like Lizzie Borden live on in the popular imagination, but young Elmer is gone. He was subjected to a period of intense scrutiny. Pundits sweated mightily to understand him, but then oblivion overtook Elmer as the pundits turned their attentions elsewhere.

Not only was Elmer denied his condign notoriety, but he was made to look ludicrous as the press attributed to him all the values of an up-and-coming liberal from Scarsdale. He was complicated, sensitive, troubled, victimized, and creative. Doubtless some of the pundits fooled around with the notion that his misdeeds came as a result of anxiety over the spread of nuclear energy or the sad condition of the whooping crane. The sense that there is something really admirable beneath the surface of a killer is an old problem with the pundits. Some of them, having never fully grown up and still secretly harboring the feeling that they are powerless children, tend easily to identify with perceived underdogs even if those dogs are trapped killers. Others are liberals smitten by what Kenneth Minogue in *The Liberal Mind* claims they never can resist, a perceived suffering situation. Others are playing God, creating what they want to create. And still others are ideologues, using the emergence of a scoundrel like young Elmer as an opportunity to prove that society is corrupt and must be radically changed. The reasoning here is illogical, but the dramatic impact of transforming the likes of young Elmer into the innocent victim of an unjust society apparently distracts readers from the story's paralogistic foundation. Today large numbers of semieducated Americans see the plight of criminals as an indication not that America is tolerant but that it is intolerant and its institutions illegitimate. Astrology also strikes them as plausible.

In the case of young Elmer, hardly had he finished confessing to his butcherings than the pundits were rushing out stories of how ironic and sadly ill-starred his life had been. Through them all inhered the suggestion that this stupefying ghoul was interesting and admirable, though sorely pressed by circumstance. The Associated Press ran a particularly memorable story entitled "Who is Elmer Henley?" With the care of a master craftsman the reporter stuffed into his story every idiotic variation of the myth of the scoundrel as victim.

Elmer Wayne Henley

Our AP poet began his fable by contrasting young Elmer's grisly achievements with an obviously contrived personality profile drawn supposedly from neighborhood reminiscences. We were given glimpses of the fabulous young Elmer as "the considerate elder of the family, trying to fill an absent father's role, going to his brothers' school to check on their progress." He is "reflective," a man whose "memories were his own," and who sought a change of cell because the boorish prisoners "were abusing him." Naturally he is "intelligent," "always gentle," and "always polite." No less an authority than his minister, the Rev. Matt Chambers, is summoned to scotch those readers inclined to snicker: "he was not different from any boy. . . . He had a deep sense of responsibility and felt he was a breadwinner." So there you are! Elmer Henley, future astronaut!

In a haunting conclusion our AP poet once again nudges our consciences, "Who Is Elmer Henley?" Well, I looked into the enigma, and according to my research this young genius, so bent on community service and self-improvement, was arrested for assault with a deadly weapon in 1971 (age fifteen). He was picked up for burglary and theft in 1972 (age sixteen). A year later he was assisting the authorities in exhuming the remains of twenty-seven children, many of whom he had admitted to torturing and murdering. All in all a mixed career, but if pushed to a judgment I believe I would find him somewhat less typical than did the Rev. Chambers.

Another memorable analysis of young Elmer's brighter side appeared in the *Los Angeles Times*. As the *Times* reported: "after Elmer was jailed in the mass murder, he [Elmer's lawyer] talked to him one day on the telephone about meeting his mother in the courtroom the next day. He said 'Will I be able to kiss mama?' " It goes without saying that the calloused authorities refused this tender request. The *Times* even per-

ceived Elmer's accomplice, a middle-aged homosexual elec-
trician, as something other than a commonplace thug. This
engaging mass-murderer was depicted as "polite, quiet, and
pleasantly harmless." Moreover he was also "nice to children." Elsewhere a reporter actually described his life as "a
modern American tragedy."

There is indeed a tragedy about all this. These men were
no-nonsense types. They went out and committed acts of real
wickedness. Few men living or dead could claim as much,
and look what the press did to them. My guess is that we would
get at least as accurate a report on the character and misdeeds
of scoundrels like Elmer if they wrote their stories themselves.
But then there would be serious questions raised over their
professional qualifications. The professionalism of an American newspaper reporter is an arcane and marvelous thing.

11

Robert Preston:
Awash in History's Wake

NO YOKEL in American history has quite so artlessly flummoxed an appointment with fame, prosperity, and power as Mr. Robert Preston, the audacious young grease monkey who became the first person ever to lead an aerial assault on the White House when he attempted to ram it with his pilfered UH–1 (Huey) helicopter. The exact date of his tryst was February 17, 1974, and, so far as my staff has been able to ascertain, Jehovah reserved that date for him with no strings attached. Nonetheless, Mr. Preston blew it. While looking a gift horse in the mouth he fell into a funk, and the wheel of history ground on. By the time he had come to his hour had passed. Back into the shadows he had slipped, there to stumble through a meaningless existence with the millions of other patheticoes who grouse about the "good fortune" of their betters.

Jehovah must have been appalled, and surely many sharp public relations men still shake their heads as they muse upon

the tidy fortune poor Mr. Preston could have earned for them.
It was as though haberdasher Harry Truman had turned down
the call to public service and continued to bankrupt himself,
or the Pope had snubbed the summons of the angels and
opened a spaghetti parlor. Not since a youthful Edward Kennedy turned his back on driver's education classes has a mortal
so thumpingly sealed his own fate. ROBERT PRESTON
. . . you will probably never hear his name again. *Au revoir,*
oaf.

What this poor fish did was, in this glorious era, well-nigh
unthinkable. He committed a mischievous and indeed felonious act and did not make the faintest gesture to embroider it
with noble purpose or high-toned symbolism. He merely
stepped from his wounded helicopter and confessed to the assembled reporters and secret servicemen: "There wasn't anything else to do"—not a word about political repression, eco-
logical suicide, or alienation and the search for one's sexuality.
Preston could have mentioned the cruel condition of our
women, the political castration of our homosexuals, the im-
pending demise of the black-footed ferret, or the heartbreak of
psoriasis. Rather, he grinned. And, though *Newsweek* described it as a "cryptic" grin, it was a grin nevertheless. Had he
possessed the astuteness to boom for any one of the aforementioned causes he would be a free man today with a gorgeous
publishing contract, a decade's lecturing engagements on the
college Chautauqua circuit, and an office in Washington paid
for by some occult rivulet of the Department of Health, Education and Welfare. Instead, he grinned.

Not only is he a grinning ignoramus, but he is also selfish.
Any of a dozen just causes could have been put over on the
American people had he but uttered a threatening declaration.
He had a two-way radio, why did he not use it? Why not a
clenched fist when he emerged from the Huey? Imagine what

would have become of the Black Panthers had they merely grinned after a shoot-up. Would Mr. Huey P. Newton ever have achieved celebrity and riches had he admitted that he shot cops and tortured fellow blacks because "there wasn't anything else to do"? Consider the rise of artsy pornography. If the aesthetes who began producing renderings of man's goatish impulses in the 1960s had stated at the outset that they wanted to create salacious movies so that they could make mounds of money, how many opportunities do you suppose we would have to appreciate sadism, bestiality, and masochism today? The pioneers of adult theater had to loosen up the Supreme Court with a few shots of the First Amendment. They had to address themselves to a worthy cause, the cause of free expression and art. Presto, progress was at hand, the greatest advance in art since John Cage heard fingernails scratch across a blackboard.

So let us wash our hands of this wretch. He committed an audacious act and fouled it with a stupid and irresponsible grin. Had he called a press conference and announced that his flight was meant to symbolize the immediate need to impeach Richard Nixon he would have made the cover of every newsweekly in the country. He could have become *Time*'s "Man of the Year." Instead he grinned and admitted to having a vacant mind. No other eminento of recent years was so foolhardy, and none had a briefer stay in the limelight.

12

Major Claude Robert Eatherly: Faith in Our Time

AS A LONGTIME ADMIRER of man's ability to believe any preposterosity that soothes him, I was especially pleased to read of the July 1, 1978, death of Major Claude Robert Eatherly, United States Army Air Corps, discharged.

Eatherly was that larcenous dissipater who claimed that, as a highly decorated World War II pilot, he had bombed Hiroshima, only to be hounded by his conscience into a postwar life of self-destructive petty crime and shiftlessness. His career as a public nuisance began in the 1950s when a newspaper reporter, gullible even by modern American standards, found him locked away in a remote Texas hoosegow. Eatherly was a born blank, but even he recognized opportunity when it tripped into his cell, note pad in hand. Rising to the occasion, Eatherly gave the reporter the marvelous tale of bunk for which he undoubtedly yearned. Eatherly claimed to have led the bombing mission over Hiroshima. It was the crowning moment in a glorious military career full of decorations for in-

Major Claude Robert Eatherly

comparable valor and savagery. He claimed to have won the Distinguished Flying Cross, and insisted that he was on his way to a lofty position in the military-industrial complex when, without warning, that moral recrudescence flared in the back of his coco. His ensuing sense of guilt transformed and enlarged him: Major Claude Robert Eatherly, the Napoleon of Hiroshima, became a drunk. He also became a petty thief, a check forger, and a peripatetic inhabitant of insane asylums, prisons, and Veterans' Administration hospitals. The newspaperman reported it all.

Overnight Eatherly was celebrated in books, plays, television dramas ("The Big Story"), and magazines—*Newsweek*'s memorable headline was "Hero in Handcuffs." Bertrand Russell expounded on Eatherly's moral significance. Progressives all over the world fought back the tears. John Wain, one of England's "Angry Young Men," composed a poem whose last lines went:

> Say nothing of love, or thanks, or penitence:
> say only "Eatherly, we have your message."*

The liberal brethren saw the heroic major's life as a frightening parable, proving the cogency of one or another of their hysterical and mysterious fears. They made him an international symbol and gave him awards like the 1962 Hiroshima Award "for outstanding contributions to world peace." Eatherly, heretofore a man of only the most modest cons, was stunned by his good fortune. Yet he soon fell in with the hoax, and in time became a creditable pontificator—despite the fact that he had never had the educational benefits of a George McGovern or a Dick Cavett.

* From John Wain, *Weep Before God*. Reprinted by permission of Curtis Brown Ltd.

Public Nuisances

Eatherly's fame was a constant threat to the counterfeit war stories he had dreamt up, and he was always having to scale them down much as our Jimmy has perforce quietly discarded so many of his own autobiographical extravagances: his close friendship with Admiral Hyman Rickover, his years as an atomic scientist. In truth, Eatherly was uniquely undecorated. He never won the Distinguished Flying Cross, never commanded the Hiroshima bombing mission, and never harmed the hair of a Japanese citizen—at least in wartime. In fact, it was subsequently divulged that Eatherly went through the entire war without having ever fired a hostile shot. Moreover, he had competed furiously, if unsuccessfully, for the honor of dropping atomic bombs at the first Bikini tests. During the Hiroshima bombing he never even saw a mushroom cloud; all he did was fly a navigation plane over the city and from thirty thousand feet report weather conditions. If he was responsible for the incineration of that fated city, so was every mechanic who ever rubbed grease into the real bomber's landing gear; so were Adam and Eve.

All this notwithstanding, the liberals strenuously perpetuated the Eatherly legend until it is now venerated by every schoolmarm. No child escapes our public school system without hearing it at least once. So deeply rooted is it in our folklore that when the *New York Times* reported Eatherly's funeral our nation's newspaper of record left the legend reverently intact: "Claude Robert Eatherly, who, as a young Army Air Corps pilot, picked a hole through the clouds over Japan in his bomber on the morning of August 6, 1945 and radioed the B-29 Enola Gay to drop its atomic bomb on Hiroshima, died of cancer last Saturday in Houston. . . . Mr. Eatherly's brother James, of Midland, Texas, told reporters: 'I can remember his waking up night after night. He said his brain was on fire. He said he could feel those people

burning.' " When questioned by writer William Bradford
Huie, Eatherly's estranged wife said she had never heard such
nocturnal cries nor had she ever heard the hero express any
anxiety or remorse over Hiroshima. They were not divorced
until 1957.

Even in death the Eatherly legend continued to grow and to
abet our more current liberal hysterias. According to the *Times*
story, one of the dead fraud's brothers "recalled that Mr. Eatherly had flown a plane through a mushroom cloud during
nuclear tests on Bikini atoll and said that he thought the flier
had suffered long-term radiation damage." Eatherly, an unshakable hypochondriac, had plagued Veterans' Administration hospitals for thirty years with his imagined afflictions. No
test ever performed on his extensively tested carcass ever
showed any evidence of "long-term radiation damage."

To believe in the saintliness of a rascal like Eatherly one had
to force from one's mind innumerable facts and revelations
and alibis. One had to have faith in absurdity. Precisely this
faith came to characterize hundreds of thousands of liberals
during the 1960s and 1970s. One can only guess at how many
other, more adroit, Eatherlies were championed by the
righteous liberals of the era. My suspicion is that dozens of
antiwar protestors, civil-rights leaders, consumerists, environmentalists, and other such activists led lives of cooked-up
heroism and blatant hypocrisy in pursuit of what appear to be
increasingly empty causes. My mind is full of memories of
terse and vaguely worded news stories like the report on the
leader of the National Welfare Rights Organization, who
drowned after a fall from his yacht. I have seen too many thick
gold watches on the wrists of "militants" and "activists" to
believe in the singularity of Eatherly. If there ever was a time
in America when more Eatherlies edified us I am unfamiliar
with it.

13

Betty Friedan and the Women of the Fevered Brow

THE MOVEMENT was born amid the sounds of the morning wash being automatically battered and dried in the laundry rooms of suburbia. The last crumbs of breakfast had been lugged away, the coffee was poured, and a scowling Miss Betty Friedan sat with the most awesome circle of women ever gathered under the roof of a modern ranch-type house. Together they deliberated, as rage feathered the linings of their bowels. The whole day yawned before them. Soon it would be back and forth, back and forth to the powder room. Coffee and housework can have that effect. These brave women were trapped with a vast expanse of desolate hours stretching out to that remote time when the kids returned from school and the idiot traipsed in with his evening paper. It was insanity, and still the infernal washing machine kept vibrating in the background. Soon the maid would be emptying it and feeding it, emptying it and feeding it. There would be telephones and shopping and God knows what all. Rosa Luxemburg had been right; so had—their genitalia notwithstanding—C. Wright Mills and Norman O. Brown. It was time to hoist the black flag. Penis envy, ha!

The women began to read, and in time they began to shout. Millions of witches had been burned in the Middle Ages, yet here we were early in the 1960s and still no inquest had been held. Not even many books on the atrocity could be found. There was much work to be done. Prodigious matriarchal societies had once flourished in the rain forests of tropic lands, yet anthropologists—some of them women—would tell no one. When asked, some would snicker; others grew impatient. Revelations like this make you think. They can be radicalizing. And by 1963 there emerged what came to be called the women's liberation movement—though on its dates there may be some dispute. Yet, let us not tarry over this issue of the movement's origins. Disputes abound in the movement, captiousness at times appearing to be the movement's *raison d'être*, and we must not let the minutiae of these disputes distract us from our inquiry. Women's liberation is probably the most successful pestilence since Prohibition, a movement that was likewise under feminine stewardship. It thrived, nourished as it was by the major philosophical current of modern America, namely self-interest, improperly understood. It is sufficient to point out that most scholars have laid the movement's origins to the 1963 publication of Miss Friedan's *The Feminine Mystique*, the book that elucidated the arcane fetters of housewifery as it had come to be practiced in the middle of the twentieth century. With its publication there appeared some remarkable blips on the sociological seismographs. Thousands, perhaps millions, of women had had enough.

These were no mere middle-class automatons, these women of the fevered brow. They were members of the intelligentsia. They were visionaries. In time they were revolutionaries. Trotsky could have learned a thing or two from them. So could Lenin. So too Zinoviev. For instance, they could have learned to achieve orgasm without recourse to the male member. They could have learned that in the twentieth century revolution starts at the kitchen sink, rages on into the bedroom, and is not assuaged by the electric dishwasher. What is more, the old Bolsheviks could have learned that though one can fundamentally dizzy a modern liberal democracy with homemade bombs, one can accomplish much more dizziness merely by being a rancorous pest. But here the lessons end, for, truth to tell, "the women" were never very deep. It is doubtful that any movement in history ever went so far on so few ideas.

What passed for ideas in the women's movement were some of the scrawniest specimens of cognition ever spied. When all the litigation and legislation is ended, when the last bloodcurdling yell is loosed from the powder room, history will note that the ideology of the modern feminist is less prepossessing or challenging than the ideology of the modern nudist. Next to the illustrious Miss Friedan, the late Mr. Maurice Parmelee, author of *The New Gymnosophy* (1927) and *Nudism in Modern Life* (1952), was an Aristotle.

Yet is it not possible that the movement threw up its pathetic ideas as a mere tactical ruse? Could the women of the fevered brow have hoped that by advancing puny ideas they might evade the attention of thinking persons and hence escape the fearful drubbing that a movement based on such flyblown premises might otherwise suffer? Certainly women are capable of learning, brilliant analysis, and sound argumentation. In our time we have seen it in the work of Hannah Arendt and Iris Murdoch to name but two. The geniuses of the women's movement confected ideas that were uniformly stupid and boring. There might indeed be a clever stratagem at

work here. If so, it was radiantly successful, for as the movement gained influence, irretrievably poisoning select regions
of our liberal polity, only rarely did a serious thinker in a
serious intellectual forum pause to give this asinine ideology
the once-over. Freedom was subtly diminished, commerce
threatened, and civility frayed. Nonetheless, in the world of
ideas women's liberation, so-called, was almost never critically
discussed. Occasionally a thoughtful writer like Midge Decter
or George Gilder would weigh in to expose the women's liberationists for the moonshiners that they were, but then there
would be silence. The welfare state, the cold war, the "social
issues" were all discussed intelligently and at length throughout the 1960s and 1970s, but women's liberation fetched no
such sustained examination from the high intellectuals. The
matter was simply too tedious and the costs too high. To question the tenets of women's liberation was to invite mayhem
and be drawn into an orgy of idiocy.

As the years sauntered by, the grumpy women kept heaving
up their imbecilic monographs: nonce books whose titles and
obsessions are today forgotten by all save a few thousand scholarly disposed lesbians and divorcées. Not one of these books attracted a careful scrutiny or lasting interest. In the more popular forums of review like the *New York Times Book Review*, it
quickly became the custom to have these imbecilic screeds
reviewed solely by female publicists of the sisterhood.
The result was an orderly patter of approbation and then oblivion. Never were serious intellectuals heard to complain; they
simply did not care to touch the stuff.

Even in the journals of ritualistic *gauchisme*, the women's
claptrap rapidly exhausted intelligent readers. It was a phenomenon to ignite amazement: even Irving Howe, even
Michael Harrington wearied of writing about women's liberation, despite the glad tidings that the movement had caused

huge misery for the bourgeois conspiracy—more, actually, than any Marxist poultice ever bootlegged into the Great Republic. The *Nation*, the *New Republic*, *Dissent*, and almost every other house of left-wing worship soon confined discussion of the movement to back pages, and then almost always to the authorship of women's liberationists.

What fleeting notice a feminist ideologue would attract was always owing to: a) the egalitarian perfumes of our time, b) the self-loathing that always seems to be licking at some of our cultural leaders, and c) outlandishness. This outlandishness, which characterized almost every single feminist idea, was to be expected, for the whole movement was based on palpable fantasy. It was the women's liberationists' seminal insight that despite the evidence of the naked eye or even of the scientifically assisted eye, woman the concave is no different from man the convex. What the feminists were saying was that a nut has the same properties as a bolt, and it was beliefs like this that made many Americanoes glad that Betty Friedan and her cohorts were revolutionaries and not mechanics or carpenters. The fact that men and women had followed different roles for thousands of years never wobbled the women of the fevered brow. Rather, they advanced this historic distinction as irrefutable evidence of a vast global plot against womenfolk. Four thousand years of recorded history only made the women all the madder and their ideas more outlandish.

For a while the women were stupendously prolific with bizarre notions: genital differences between men and women are culturally induced; twelve thousand years ago women ruled the earth; female-male relationships were based on rape; women are more petite than the male of the species because of male oppression; war exists because men run governments. Every season brought a new liberationist genius spouting a goofball idea whose lifespan would be about equal to that of a summer fly, and for every one autumn would come. No one would even pause to bury the carcasses or to notice the dark hole into which each genius disappeared. What happened to them is unrecorded. Doubtless some found positions teaching humbug on college campuses. Others suffered worse fates. I remember one turning up on New York City's welfare roles, and there were at least two who made it back into the klieg light only when they were arrested for shoplifting—a matter the disciples of Dr. Freud will doubtless make much to-do about.

The movement was always a journey into unreason and a flight from the responsibilities and liberties that had opened to women after World War II. These increased liberties and responsibilities came mainly through technological and economic advances. Their debt to politics was only very subtle, having to do with the whole sweep of our western culture and having almost nothing to do with specific political activity. Political haranguing came after the fact, that is, after technological innovations beckoned women into realms from which, heretofore, they had been absent. To be sure, women were increasingly uneasy at mid-century, and their unease was caused by liberal ideas and the development of industrial capitalism. The first deauthorized the realms of women, and the second rendered their homes economically less important. So here society was faced with an increase in liberty, prosperity, and anxiety, and America's women of the fevered brow responded with a grandiose temper tantrum. In their tirades they called themselves progressive and enlightened.

Yet, notwithstanding the small matter that their ideas were preposterous and that serious thinkers dismissed them as a curiosity of American popular culture, the women's liberationists were, as with so many other vulgar enthusiasms of the recent years, full of high ideals and intellectual pretense. Unfortunately, the basic stupidity of their intellects kept foozling them. When it came time to suit their actions to their thoughts they would come up with travesties like the following, quoted from a 1976 press release of the feminist National Organization for Women:

> Jan Crawford, a feminist writer and massage therapist, will conduct a program on Healing with Massage on Thursday, October 14th, at 7 p.m. in the NOW Center, 47 E. 19th St.
>
> Ms. Crawford's presentation will include a discussion of the problems women have with giving and receiving in addition to a demonstration of massage techniques that are helpful in relieving stress-related ailments such as headaches. Audience participation will be encouraged.
>
> Programs and meetings are held every Thursday evening in the NOW Center.

As to the quality of Miss Crawford's literary artistry, I am unable to judge, having—let me be frank—never heard of her. But as to the quality of her mind . . . well, can you imagine Diana Trilling giving a lecture on the healing science of massage? Nonetheless you can be sure that the women gathered at the NOW Center full of high purpose and cerebral snootiness. It was characteristic.

Not only did the women of the fevered brow fail to come up with one lasting book or one notable sage, they also failed to produce òne journal of opinion with any standing in the intellectual community whatsoever. Every movement of any serious philosophical import has a journal or two that, given its philosophic borders, displays learning and rigor and is looked to as an intellectual source. What journal do the women of the fevered brow have? They have *Ms.*, a journal that appears in supermarkets everywhere. This is a rather telling detail. Communists, Zionists, conservatives, and so forth

Betty Friedan

all have intellectually respectable journals. The women's
movement has *Ms.* No description of this idiot sheet can cap-
ture its full fragrance. The most clinically perfect description
of it would inevitably leave me open to charges of exaggera-
tion, an allegation that might ruin my standing as a writer.
And so I have decided it best to serve up a characteristic collection of passages gathered from *Ms.* over the years. Draw your
own conclusions.

In reviewing a book entitled *Our Blood: Prophecies and Dis-
courses on Sexual Politics*, a *Ms.* reviewer stated in the February, 1977 number: "She scrutinizes historical and psychological
issues, including female masochism, rape, the slavery of
women in 'Amerika,' and the burning of nine million witches
during the Middle Ages. Then she calls for—insists upon,
really—a complete cultural transformation, the rooting out of
sex roles from our society." The book under review was written
by a Miss Andrea Dworkin, and luckily a specimen of her
thought was contained in the December, 1976 number: "In
fucking and in reproduction, sex and economics cannot be
separated. The man takes a body that is not his, claims it, sows
his so-called seed, reaps a harvest—he colonizes a female
body, robs it of its natural resources, controls it, denies it
freedom and self-determination so that he can continue to
plunder it, moves on at will to conquer other land which appears more verdant and alluring. Radical feminists call this exclusively male behavior 'phallic imperialism' and see in it the
origin of all other forms of imperialism." *Mein Gott!* It makes
you want to burn every bed in America.

Ms. is not only full of commentary on political economy, it
also contains commentary on the arts. In the August, 1975
number, the movies of the illustrious Pam Grier were reviewed: "In 'Foxy Brown' she avenges the cold-blooded slaying
of her brother and boyfriend by castrating the villain, putting

113

Public Nuisances

his penis in a jar filled with pickling juice, and making a present of it to his girl friend. . . . [Ms. Grier's] are the only films to come out of Hollywood in a long time to show us a woman who is independent, resourceful, self-confident, strong, and courageous. Above all, they are the only films to show us a woman who triumphs!"

Of course, those who write for *Ms.* are no more idiotic than those who read it. Fortunately, *Ms.* publishes vast fields of correspondence and in so doing gives us some sense of the rank-and-file women's liberationist.*

Consider:

I just read Eve Babitz's article, "My Life in a 36DD Bra" (April, 1976). Fantastic! I was amazed by the similarity of our experiences—right down to both of us being "Late Bloomers" and having the same bra size. . . .

Finally at the age of 22 I am getting used to the size of my breasts and learning to take in stride those people who seem to be unable to see anything of me beyond them.

——— ———

Cedar Rapids, Iowa

Ahhhh! The joys of womanhood in a sexist society! To have the power to turn men to mush by virtue of our 36DD breasts. Now that's strength!

How elevating it was to read, in a feminist publication, such insightful and comforting affirmations. Yes, men do judge a woman's attractiveness by the amount of fatty tissue that is piled up on her chest. . . . Yes, big "tits" can be a woman's most valuable possession and should be exploited to their fullest extent. Yes, there is some discomfort involved: the inconvenience of wearing "disguises," the painful bursting of your illusion when you discover your leg man really wanted "knockers" all the time. "Sex objects," you say, "depersonalization," "degradation"? Why,

* All letters appeared in *Ms.* magazine, August 1976, August 1977, and August 1978.

with all the attention our big tits attract, who has the time to notice?

———   ———

Toronto, Ont., Canada

Why is it important for women to use "dirty words"? . . .

I think a female's use of words abusive to females *defuses* them. *Our* use takes away the power of the words to damage us. They are no longer tools with which to shock and humiliate. And it's fun, after all these years of proper servitude to a restrictive language code, to bounce them all over the walls and hear not only their echoes but the shock waves from men.

While our use of words like "fuck" may indeed shock men, it also removes the fangs from the words men customarily use to keep us in our place. The woman who objects to their use feels that it is offensive to her, to our "image," and beneath the "holy state of womanhood" to hear them. Such women are sitting ducks for abuse at any time.

Let us break down this system of abuse—take the power to hurt from the particular vocabulary list. In fact, fuck it!

Then we can begin to talk again.

———   ———

Durham, N.C.

I strongly object to the superficial, flippant tone of Lindsy Van Gelder's article, "Hot Off the Feminist Presses: New Journals" (November, 1977).

I was particularly upset at the misrepresentation of *Woman-Spirit* magazine. . . . In my close to three-year relationship with *WomanSpirit*, and Ruth and Jean Mountaingrove, its caretakers, I have found the magazine thought-provoking, inspirational, and comforting. . . .

The woman Van Gelder referred to as being a sort of final last straw is a personal friend of mine who does, indeed, converse with trees, and two in particular are her special friends. I have been known to talk with tree beings myself, and many other women I know also do so.

Any hope for a sane future that will lead us out of the mess

we're in will lie in opening ourselves up with joy and understanding to the many other realities present in the universe. Talking with trees is but one way. Once we open ourselves to the
knowledge of the life forms with which we share this planet, the
old mind-think of patriarchal culture no longer holds as much
power over us.

—— ——

Portland, Ore.

The movement never made very deep furrows in Europe,
and in the Third World it was almost unheard of. Still, it is a
testimonial to the ravenous ignorance of the movement that in
the late 1960s and early 1970s women's liberationists would
always be rising up from their conventions, stentoriously declaring their solidarity with the sisters of the Third World,
many of whom lived in daily dread of ugly spirits and black
magic, to say nothing of the fearful sough of an electric washing machine. At times some forward-thinking pedagogue full
of idealism and self-contempt would leap from the crowd and
shout his approval. With especial delight I remember a Dr.
George Stade of Columbia University, who, in praising one of
the passing classics of the movement, intoned: "Reading it is
like sitting with your testicles in a nutcracker"—an experience
that for Dr. Stade could have ended in brain damage.

Yet in the end it has to be said that if the movement was not
an intellectual triumph it was somewhat of a social success,
sending millions of women off on a brave quest for success in
the arts, the realms of the intellect, the Fortune 500, and politics. Where their quest will end will not be known for a generation. Great strides are supposedly being made by the women
of the fevered brow in persuading their fellow women of suburbia to scotch the washing machine and escape their children. Unfortunately, their children cannot escape them, and
it is the genius of the movement not to allow anyone else to es-

cape them. The women have already established it as their constitutional right to inflict themselves on anyone who attracts their malevolent attention. And the menfolk of the Republic continue to snore and to hope the pestilence will pass on. Such are the fearsome oppressors against whom Betty Friedan and her legions admonish us.

PART
III
THE PUBLIC NUISANCE
AS POLITICIAN

14

Bella Abzug:
A Good Word for Hate

IF YOU FOLLOW the gutters of New York's Fifth Avenue to the south, past the fashionable shops, past Saint Patrick's Cathedral, down past the old Flatiron Building, and beyond, eventually you will come upon a neighborhood where it makes little difference whether you crawl in the gutter or walk upright on the sidewalk. Here everyone is treated equally; gutter life and sidewalk society merge into one coarse throng. This was once the neighborhood of third-rate writers and artists; it is now the neighborhood of failed culturati, of the lumpen proletariat, of degenerates, addicts, and Iowa runaways reborn by an apocalyptic encounter with J. D. Salinger. Superstition is rampant, as is general ignorance, sloth, and dudgeon. Appropriately enough this was the launching site for Mrs. Martin Abzug. This is Greenwich Village; here Bella Abzug learned about mankind and vowed to do something about it.

What she decided to do was to become "an activist," by

Public Nuisances

which she obviously meant a special kind of politico: one who combines the coffeehouse existentialist's virtues of being "agonized" and "emotional" with the traditional pol's virtues of duplicity, avarice, and sagacity in the art of fleecing the public. All this and more she related in her published diary modestly titled *Bella!* It was an odd book whose style suggested the collaboration of a J. Walter Thompson ad hack and a mass murderer. One reading of it planted within me the profound conviction that Bella Abzug was not just your run-of-the-mill bombastic crank. She was a devoted opponent of civil liberties. The American political system was not her political system; at election time she yearned for the sound of bones breaking.

The haranguer from New York's 20th Congressional District gained her understanding of human nature in a neighborhood composed of the most demented elements from academe, Hell's Kitchen, and Scarsdale. Once in the House of Representatives she would take long swims in the Capitol natatorium, floating placidly on the only set of water wings ever seen in those august parts. But in her head always there floated visions of her grotesque constituents. As she trundled down the halls of the Capitol she dreamt of vast war protests, even when there was no war. She envisioned long lines of starving Americans, though there were no such Americans. She saw an invincible army of Amazons streaming out of some mountainous province in the American interior, eager to right the wrongs daily being perpetrated in the kitchens and bedrooms of the Republic; but there was no such army, no such province, and no such injustice.

These realities, however, had no impact on the legendary "activist." Present to her the defense budget, and her ears filled with the long-dead diatribe of some lunatic sage from Washington Square. Discuss social policy, and her ears resounded with the *Internationale*. Mention the Chamber of Commerce, and she reached for a Molotov cocktail. As Madame Abzug saw it, *The Federalist Papers* were glaringly deficient. Not one of them ever mentioned the positive aspects of pure hate, and as she understood it hate was the key to political action in any democracy. From September 1976 to February 1977 she lost three straight elections, yet on she roared excoriating an America that ceased to exist sometime during the administration of Theodore Roosevelt—some thought she had the Kaiser's Germany in mind.

Hate was her afflatus. Her education may have given her a wobbly capacity for analytical thought, but it undoubtedly gave her a robust capacity for hate. Thought corrupts the serious activist; hate energizes, focuses, and improves him. As politicoes go Madame Abzug was not widely informed. In fact there were vast areas of American life about which she remained prodigiously in the dark, but her performance as an activist was all the better for her ignorance. It gave punch to her tirades about capitalists, generals, and the male of the species. What intellection she devoted to the American scene was prefigured by the popular leftist belief that lives led in insane asylums are not very different from lives led in Omaha. According to this perspective the average Americano is probably a thief, his children depraved, and his wife a seething victim of four thousand years of inexplicable and impregnable oppression. The American system is an oligarchy, alive with a multitude of conspiracies. Many Americans suffer mental illness due to the profit motive (*incitamentum pecuniarium*), and every year capitalism thwarts millions of noble aspirations, jails thousands of noble aspirants, and poisons one of the Great Lakes. If the plain folk remain numb to these threats, something truly untoward and violent will occur anon . . . perhaps sooner. Even then there is no guarantee that America can be reformed into the tidy glory that is Cuba or mainland

Public Nuisances

China or some other Marxist paradise. How to bring Americans around to an understanding of this state of emergency? Here a belief in the positive uses of hate was simply not enough; and so Madame Abzug provided the lunatic left with a praxis at once economical and easy to use. To the political philosophy of arrant hate she welded the political technique of the blood-curdling yell.

Madame Abzug was not only the most respected proponent of hate at large in the Republic in the 1960s and 1970s, she was also the most seasoned rabble-rouser since Father Charles E. Coughlin. She was a born shouter. Her ample jowls were made for scowling. No beauty queen was ever more munificently endowed for her role than was Madame Abzug for hers. The constantly shifting eyes lurking beneath a forehead of concrete, the iron jaw, the thick arms bashing at the air. Not even Mussolini was more perfectly cast. And her style of dress? *Ugly*! Some laughed, but they missed the mark. She was a woman who really knew how to dress. Her dress harmonized exquisitely with the ugliness of her message. It would have been absurd and dysfunctional for her to bellow out her rage attired as Jacqueline Onassis or Nancy Reagan. From the turn of her ankles to the rasp in her voice she was a demagogue divinely constructed.

While in Congress Madame Abzug used all of her swell gifts so adroitly that hardly a solon ever challenged her gasconade. She would lumber in, and they would sweat. One roar loosed from her leathery lungs would shut down every professional patriot on the floor of the House. Two roars would send them diving for shelter. Never was she asked to provide evidence for her canards about American enormities. Only rarely was she pressed to defend the harebrained legislation she confected. And she never had to face up to the truth that her panaceas

Bella Abzug

were not only not progressive, but they were also not democratic, not egalitarian, and not humane.

Taken one with another they amounted to the old Marxist
flim-flam. Madame Abzug would have had all Americans living like Cambodians. For her to get away with appropriating
the label liberal was to make a mockery of the Truth-in-Adver-
tising Act. She was a straightforward totalitarian, susceptible to
every quibble the Marxist has with a free society, eager for
every statist intrusion into the lives of private citizens, and utterly indifferent to the spreading dark age of tyranny that stalks
every continent.

She was violent in her denunciations of Chilean misanthropes and South African racists, but did she ever enter a dissenting opinion against the Communist thugs whose billy clubs are sovereign over 40 percent of the world? Did she ever speak up as democracy was being snuffed out by the tin-pot generalissimos of the Third World? I have not heard of it.

The closest she ever came was in her 1976 speech commemorating Captive Nations Week, and then the dictatorship she chose to upbraid was India! Captive Nations Week itself is an empty tradition amongst our politicoes, who yearly observe it to ingratiate themselves with constituents of the ethnic persuasion. The observance must always have been a particularly painful occasion for her, given the identity of the Captor. But in 1976 she outdid herself. Imagine! The Eastern Europeans were being policed and hounded; Africans were being beaten, jailed, and deported; parts of Southeast Asia had been turned into a vast torture chamber; and the legendary activist scolded India! What was even more remarkable was that throughout the entire speech not once did she mention the Soviet Union or one of the captive nations. Instead she ran through a few arpeggios of left-liberal platitudes and concluded in her traditional manner, inveighing against the great dictatorships of this century: South Vietnam, Nazi Germany, and the United States.

Only with His Excellency Andrew Young or the majority of constituents in Madame Abzug's old district do such excesses go unremarked. Of course, Madame Abzug has always provided excesses in great variety. For instance, she did not merely favor abortion, she loved it. To have heard her talk of it one would have thought abortion the culmination of romantic love, an operation of aesthetic and metaphysical beauty, limited solely by the misfortune that it as yet cannot be experienced by men. Yet, on second thought, such a limitation would not have caused her too much unease, for another of

her excesses was manifested in the area of male-female relations. She was against them. Apparently she felt that women
should have as little to do with men as possible. Madame
Abzug was one of those feminists whose apparent enthusiasm
for women derived from a basic hatred of men—though from
all available evidence she did not like women all that much
either.

Fundamentally, Madame Abzug was a hater. Informed by
quackery of a particularly freakish left-wing variety, inflamed
by a hatred of reality, and yearning for the tidiness of some
Marxist paradise, she shouted her way into the minds of voters
everywhere. But times changed, and Bella did not.

In January 1978 the estimable *New York Post* found Bella to
be the most popular woman in New York. One month later
she was beaten for a New York City congressional seat by an
actual Republican, and so Congress was denied a leading
member of an increasingly important American political
grouping: the disloyal opposition. Doubtless she will be heard
from again.

15

Hubert Humphrey:
A Victim of Decency

"LIBERALISM," a prominent American historian is given to proclaiming, "is the institutionalization of decency." This estimate I lay before you with a heart full of goodwill and sweetness. I am as free of derision and bile as a newborn babe, citing the above lilt solely because it so neatly sums up the creed of millions of feverishly busy Americanoes drawn from the higher orders and devoted to lives full of secular grace. Only a very low fellow would scoff at such a noble devotion. Yet the dissolute condition of "liberalism" in the late 1970s suggests that the slavish pursuit of decency carries with it some peril. Soon or late an obsession for decency is as corrupting as the obsessive pursuit of mammon or of Capitol Hill cuties. The case of Hubert Horatio Humphrey, deceased, entombed, and glorified, is a case in point. Born in modest circumstances, he became the paradigmatic modern liberal, the paradigmatic modern pol, and a much richer man than his rhetoric or his redistributionist policies would lead one to expect, clever fellow.

Hubert's initial stint on behalf of his fellow man was undertaken during the 1930s from behind the counter of the Humphrey Drug Store. These were relatively quiet years for Hubert. True, no customer ordered a cherry coke without suffering a hyperbolic peroration on the weather or on Eastern bankers. Nonetheless, by hindsight we can see that in those days he was practically inert, even reticent. He ventured forth briefly to study at the Capitol College of Pharmacy in Denver, Colorado, and later at the University of Minnesota, but for the most part he remained quiescent for a full thirty years. Then this late bloomer bloomed and with a yelp.

I lay the whole clamorous transformation to his dip into higher education. Frankly, the life of the mind fetched him, and, as with so many like him, it transformed him into a life-long denizen of the public sector. He earned an M. A. at Louisiana State University, taught government, and studied further at the University of Minnesota. The longer he stewed in book learning the more volatile his ingredients became. Suddenly in 1941 he erupted in a frenzy of energy the like of which has rarely been witnessed in this splendid Republic or any other. By 1945 the sunny pharmacist from Huron, South Dakota, had served in over half a dozen government bureaucracies, including the WPA and the War Manpower Commission. He united the Democratic and Farmer-Labor parties, became mayor of Minneapolis, and, while moonlighting amongst the professionally decent, cofounded Americans for Democratic Action. By 1948 Hurricane Hubert was gusting into Washington, a bona fide U. S. senator, a colossus, who for twenty-four years did not cease in his locutions or his frantic schemes for the advancement of decency. From 1965 to 1968 he served as vice-president. He won the 1969 Democratic presidential nomination, lost to Richard Nixon, took two years off to teach, and in 1970 again entered the Senate. Four times he lunged for the presidency. Twice he stalked the vice-presidency. In all these years he distinguished himself as the most ebullient, garrulous, and energetic defender of decency ever hatched. He championed many good causes, some actually worthwhile, but from the day he exited the Humphrey Drug Store never again did he labor in private enterprise—aloofness from the private sector being an almost mandatory condition for the pursuit of decency. Yet a life in the public sector need not leave one in poverty or even in middle-class anxiety. Shortly after Hubert's exit for heavenly parts it was divulged that this life-long inhabitant of the public trough had amassed vast sums, possibly millions, in blind trusts fastidiously hidden from prying eyes and bequeathed to his wife, his children, and nine of his ten grandchildren. Hubert always said that poverty was his specialty, and as with many of America's poverty specialists among his real specialties was learning how to avoid it.

The degree to which Hubert devoted his life to decency and the degree to which it corrupted him can best be assayed from reading his astonishing memoir, *The Education of a Public Man*. It is a document strikingly characteristic of late 1970s liberalism: full of elevated sentiments, contradictory solemnities, superficial thought, misinformation, obsolete analysis, and partisanship so plangent and unyielding that upon finishing it I suddenly saw Miss Sara Jane Moore in a new light. If Hubert's opponents were as devoid of virtue as he claims, then surely taking a shot at one of them is not that difficult to understand. According to Hubert, his opponents worked not only for unvirtuous policies, but they worked from unvirtuous motives. Quite possibly Miss Moore was a humanitarian only a few degrees more ardent than Hubert himself.

Hubert Humphrey

From *The Education of a Public Man* Hubert emerges as a thoroughly modern pol and a proponent of the kind of liberalism that took root in the 1930s, reached full bloom in the 1960s, and now holds on tenaciously—and absurdly—against a changing climate. Hubert's sclerotic liberalism has become so sure of its monopoly on virtue that it now vitiates its fine and historic service of raising up a standard of justice for all, increasing freedom, and extending opportunity to those without money or hope. As year chases year it grows in pretense and hysteria even as its nostrums decline in power and pertinence. Liberalism's agedness aside, Hubert's incessant politicking rendered him in the end a ravenous self-promoter utterly incapable of deliberation. He began his career with a keen intellect and a high-grade sensibility, but in the end he was left launching flummeries about "the politics of joy" and actually drawing meaning from such wind. He hoped to govern America according to this infantile canon. Imagine what James Madison would think. Even Eleanor Roosevelt might find the term indigestible. As for Hubert's fabled liberality, consider the fact that in 495 pages of memoir he ascribed not one noble motive or admirable value to one political opponent. Such is the toll that decency took on this public man.

From Hubert's memoir one sees that he dragged himself through the 1960s always smiling on the outside, often sniffling on the inside, and never learning anything. The leftists who heaved boluses of nitrogenous material at him and favored him with other discourtesies were poisoned by hate, he assures us. Yet where they came from, why they acted so shockingly, what became of them, and what could or should have been done with them never ignite his interest. It will relieve many of his readers to hear that the demonstrators numbered "only a few," but I wonder if even the decency cabal still swallows the tosh about how the cops instigated violence in Chicago in 1968. Hubert believed it, despite cynical confessions later made by radicals like Jerry Rubin, and he believed much more.

He believed that nothing critical was ever written about Great Society programs, and that there rose up no controversy over the usefulness of vast collectivist schemes to solve social problems. At least in his memoir he never indicates he has heard tell of such rumblings, and he never reveals any disposition to discuss these programs in a critical spirit. His treatment of Model Cities is instructive. Christopher DeMuth, a scholar with wide experience in urban studies, has written that Model Cities "was the most unequivocal failure of all the 'Great Society' programs." Critical literature about the program is continuing to expand, including two scholarly studies, *The Politics of Neglect* (Cambridge: The MIT Press, 1975) and *Between the Idea and the Reality* (Boston: Little, Brown & Co., 1975). Yet Hubert proudly steps forward, acknowledges the large role he played in its passage, swats at those who doubted, and ends full of hosannas, leaving his readers to believe Model Cities the most stupendous governmental thrust since the Emancipation Proclamation. That the program became an enormous botch, costing some three billion dollars, causing grave confusion at all levels of government, and eventually being sepulchered into special revenue-sharing grants, Hubert never mentions. The whole thing is palmed off as unassailable, and herein lies another example of the corruption of decency.

However, the most flagrant examples of decency's corruptive force come not in Hubert's failure to face up to error but in his failure to extend a serving of decency to those who disagreed with him, especially those to his right. As with all devotees of decency Mr. Humphrey talks constantly about compassion, candor, largeness of spirit, and so forth, yet when he turns to the loyal opposition Mr. Humphrey apparently does not believe in equal protection of the platitude.

Certainly there is little compassion in a notation he made after a telephone conversation with Richard Nixon the day after the 1968 election: "He's gracious. That's about it. To lose to Nixon. Ye gods! No warmth, no strength, no emotion, no spirit. No heart. Politics of the computer." Upon further meditation there is not much intelligence here either. Can a man without warmth or heart or spirit be gracious? And how essential to statecraft is "emotion"? For that matter all these qualities Hubert yearns for in a president are not much different from the qualities needed to win the Kentucky Derby. I can make no sense of such vaporings.

During his last years waspish recollections filled his mind. His memoir abounds with them, right up to its final page where he returns to the hellish Nixon for a final judgment, a judgment that is so sophistical and unkind that my guardian angel nudges me to quote it in full: "When the transcripts of the White House tapes were released, I was appalled at their emptiness, their lack of concern with public policy, their casual corruption of the democratic ideal. I have talked with four Presidents during my career in Washington and to the people around them. I was not close enough to Eisenhower to know his private language, but Presidents Truman, Kennedy, and Johnson were as capable of similar crudities of language as Nixon. But all of them loved their country; their failures, ineptitudes, fallibilities were mitigated by a feeling for what America is all about. That love shone through; their concern for improving the condition of our people, however they conceived it, was real." Poor Nixon, Hubert leaves him a man without a country. There is a prodigious indulgence, an awful deception going on here. There is a meanness that is really rather stunning, coming from a man who, in death, was apotheosized for his humanity.

Let me not be misread. I believe that Hubert Humphrey at the outset was indeed decent. To the end he remained, in a stunted way, an intelligent, conscientious man whose regard for decency could edify us all. His courageous battle against Communism in the late forties and his life-long devotion to civil rights showed his superior mettle. The only worthwhile chapter in his memoir is his chapter on the 1964 civil rights bill. Yet even here, in his finest hour, he shows a stunted magnanimity and little candor. Coolness toward civil rights from labor was excusable because labor "had been concerned with other questions: housing, education, economics, medical care." But a similar coolness when spied in "the business community" is rebuked a paragraph later for "its old, simplistic rhetoric about the sanctity of 'property rights' as opposed to human rights." Did Hubert forget the bigotry of the construction unions? Was he only capable of remembering the bigotry of businesses? A life devoted to the institutionalization of decency will have that sad effect on a man.

Hubert set out to be a public man in 1941; he had two marks against him: modern politics and the decency urge. Early in his career something about him moved the renowned political scientist, Professor Charles Hyneman, to advise that he make the Senate his home, even as Calhoun and Webster had before him. Alas, Hyneman was expecting too much from American political life in this century. Modern American politics, populated as it is with virtuous ideologues and frenzied self-promoters, has no place for a Webster. Dignity and deliberation vanished from the Senate years ago.

How far short of the Senate's great men Hubert fell can be seen in *The Education of a Public Man,* the most comprehensive collection of his thoughts on record. The book took some seven years to write. Originally he undertook it "to instruct future generations," but as the years rolled on it obviously was turned into just another political device. Hubert thought he could use it with its fashionable denunciations and sonorities to win the presidency in 1976. By the time it was published he was mortally ill and harboring only a pathetic hope for the White House.

It is sad that the last testimony of this modern political giant turned out to be so puny and that the modern political career has to be so shabby. Yet sadder still are the depredations decency has committed against liberalism. America has been left with a liberalism that is no longer liberal and with liberal politicians who have insurmountable difficulty being decent.

16

Richard Milhous Nixon and the Serenade in B-Flat

RICHARD MILHOUS NIXON, 5 feet 10 inches, 165 pounds, Caucasian, male, no distinguishing features. Though a man as common as anything on display in a Sears catalogue, he rose steadily to become the most widely reviled man in American history. Have I overegged the pudding? Well then, suggest to me his equal; from all history bring one forward. Even a Will Durant, even a Toynbee, would be hard pressed to find an analogue. Popular journalists resort to the name Nixon to galvanize feelings that remain at rest even when the name Stalin is mentioned. The phobia Nixon stimulates in millions of America's most virtuous and enlightened citizens is impossible to exaggerate, and this seems to be true of people all over the world. From 1970 to 1975, a poll conducted by Mme. Tussaud's Waxworks found him to be among the five most hated and feared men in history. In 1975 only Field Marshal Idi Amin Dada and the late Adolph Hitler surpassed him. Count Dracula tied him, and Jack the Ripper finished a poor fifth.

How is it that the father of Tricia and Julie has earned such disesteem? Is it for his wicked deeds: prosaic lies endlessly repeated, eavesdropping, the bombing of Cambodian progressives, the harassment of North Vietnam's liberal democrats, those brummagem uniforms he ordered for the White House guards? Surely they do not compose the *corpus delicti*. Discreditable acts they are indeed, but there must be more to the Nixon legend than this. Not even Benedict Arnold, not even Anita Bryant is so hotly scorned. Hows come?

When one studies Nixon's public career—his first yelps in Congress; the sobs and growls of his vice-presidential years; the sonorities, the scowls, the whines of presidential greatness—when one studies his opponents—their increasing alarm, their jeremiads, their snifflings, and the eerie regularity with which their reasonable objections metamorphosed into ridiculosities—it grows ever more apparent that this is not a typical political struggle. Rather it is an incomparable succession of bizarreries so traumatizing as to be explicable only in terms numenous and diabolical.

Everything about the man suggests palpable weirdness. Mention his name and millions of Americans leap to their feet yelling. Some, truth to tell, have their hands over their hearts. Others have their hands at their throats. They gurgle. They report hearing wild dogs barking and maidens sobbing. Not infrequently they end their lives shouting helplessly from the Freudian couch. Even in American politics such doings are unusual. It is my considered judgment that in the very White House where such giants as Lyndon Johnson and the sainted Kennedy brought their immense dignity, wisdom, and integrity, the Commoner from Whittier suffered diabolical infestation, and no one tried to help. Poor Nixon, everything he

Public Nuisances

touched grew fangs and let out a howl: welfare reform, a generation of peace, an unbalanced budget. In Nixon's hands all such noble aspirations went sinister. "Tory men and liberal policies are what have changed the world," he buoyantly proclaimed, and his plan for a guaranteed annual income was promptly slaughtered in the Congress. Domestic advisers like Daniel Patrick Moynihan paled; they had never seen liberals act so strangely. Yet such wonders would continue, and in time the miraculous destructiveness of the Nixon touch would become a legend.

Hugh Kenner has said that Nixon should not have been president on aesthetic grounds. It is an observation abounding with truth and stimulative of hitherto unimagined hopes for the presidency. Yet I have always contained my objections to more immediate concerns. Nixon should not have been president for reasons of public health and safety. His presence causes too much distress. In fact I suspect that over the years the untimely deaths of hundreds, perhaps thousands, of America's most upright citizens can be laid to a Nixon press conference, a UPI photograph of the man with his dog, or any of a myriad of other Nixonian apparitions. For instance, Nixon was campaigning strenuously just before the death of Paul Goodman, and during his 1970 European junket we lost Janis Joplin. I take it as a mark of the enormous strength of that great and good man, Alger Hiss, that he survived the entire Nixon presidency. His gaunt mug and watery eyes tell us much, however, about the suffering he endured throughout the "New American Revolution," the "New Federalism," the "opening to China," Julie's "wedding," and all the other dubious public relations stunts. If we were really serious about health care in America, particularly as it pertains to the cardiovascular systems and the nervous systems of our quasi-liberal brethren, I would have thought that we would have passed an amendment to the United States Constitution barring Nixon from further participation in public life and prohibiting his name from ever being mentioned in public forums. By law, scholarly books would refer to him only by euphemism.

The astonishing misfortune that befalls those who come into contact with Nixon is a riveting reminder of the power the occult has played in his life. Whether friend or foe, one steps from his presence and as likely as not the sky falls in. It is uncanny. The closer one's contact with him, the greater one's peril. His friends suffer bankruptcy, the loss of dozens of IQ points, broken spirits, and, with astounding frequency, the calaboose. His enemies suffer similar calamities. I can count three who have been assassinated and several who have been maimed. Dignity, well-being, and soundness of mind so often depart after a close brush with the man that I have no doubt his career is more comprehensible to a medieval mystic ensconced in a cave than to a modern rationalist with all his books and analytical gear.

Most spectacularly there was the late President Kennedy. Not only was he the first modern president shot from ambuscade, but he died under circumstances that still excite morbid speculation. His instantaneous apotheosis proved only to be a diabolical prank, making his eventual fall all the more ignominious. It was idolatry contrived from a presidency of singular mediocrity and a life of stunning sham. Nevertheless, soon the facts made their debut: petty political fixing, ineptitude as grandiose as his oratory, a whole family of pinheads and rascals. Floozies began stepping forward from every trailer camp in America, coyly testifying to their personal involvement with what the suave president had cockily called "class." The revelations dragged his repute from nadir to undreamt of nadir, and soon there was a movement to remove his pictures from the Catholic schools of Iowa.

Today the scholars are at work. Nothing can stop them, and within a decade his policies will be the most discredited of any president's since Hoover. His reputation will thud into that dark hole which for more than half a century has been the domicile of Warren Gamaliel Harding alone. Nor was Kennedy's widely esteemed young staff immune from the Nixon touch. After propitious beginnings they all blew up, vamoosing from politics burdened with debts and the shakes. Remember the sad cases of O'Donnell, Salinger, Sorensen, and so forth—from bathos to pathos. Had the Boy President of the 1960s run against any other Republican doubtless he would be with us today, and his administration would have been enormously more creditable. Did Pat Brown fare much better? Upon beating Nixon for the California governorship in 1962, he rapidly became a laughingstock, and it is now apparent that fate dealt him an idiot for a son.

What of Nixon's later opponents? With surprising constancy they are sick, dead, convicted of low deeds, under threat of conviction, banished, or absurd. The friends and associates of Richard Nixon have already, and in unusually large numbers, had the prison door clank behind them. Now begin the tribulations of his enemies. The column of petty malefactors and suspects straggles forward. Remember the late Senator Joseph M. Montoya of the Watergate Spectacular? Remember the Rt. Hon. Carl Albert? Why did they abscond from the limelight so hastily? Where are they now? Think well on the cyclones that struck the gorgeous careers of the Rt. Hon. Wayne Hays and the voluptuous Wilbur Mills. Then there was Senator Talmadge of the Senate Watergate Committee and then Senator Brooke, the first Republican to call for

Nixon's exit. Suddenly in the summer of 1978 both were struck by lightning. What will become of the blubbering Speaker O'Neill? Will he join the Rt. Hon. Richard T. Hanna, the Rt. Hon. Cornelius Gallagher, the Rt. Hon. Frederick W. Richmond, poor ex-Congressman Allan T. Howe, and the Rt. Hon Charles C. Diggs? Meditate on the chances of the Rt. Hon. Daniel J. Flood, and is there any hope at all for the Rt. Hon. Joshua Eilberg who, as a member of the House Judiciary Committee, observed: "our citizens are afraid that if they take a position on a political issue their telephones will be tapped, their mail opened, and their tax returns audited as a means of punishment. This result makes it imperative that Richard Nixon be impeached"? Nearly fifty congressmen from the Watergate era were in its aftermath suddenly indicted or forced to lie low. Even John Doar, Esq., chief investigator for the House Judiciary Committee during its impeachment hearing, was of a sudden painfully wriggling under the eye of a U.S. Attorney.

An astonishing number of the leading celebs of the Watergate Spectacular saw their careers evaporate. What has become of the renowned Woodward and Bernstein? Neither of them could write. Their only talent as journalists was their ability to answer crank calls in the night from whom no one knows, and the boys are not telling—at least not until the price is right. Neither of these hinds has done anything remarkable since Nixon's last helicopter flight, and I contest the notion that they ever did do anything all that remarkable except hog the show right up to the last limits of the plausible. What became of John Dean or Senator Daniel K. Inouye? My guess is they are both afflicted with some obscure and horrible disease, and never to be heard from again. And forget not that ancient gasbag, Sam Ervin, illustrious constitutional expert. He slipped so deeply into obscurity so rapidly that the American Express company exploited his instant anonymity in a television ad featuring him and Barry Goldwater's running mate as two typical nonentities urgently in need of American Express cards—a fitting testimonial to the lasting achievement of Watergate.

Watergate, of course, is the most catastrophic instance of the Nixon touch. Heretofore Nixon had dizzied only individuals; now he stultified and laid low an entire nation. Watergate led to the election of the most ill-prepared president of this century and to the hitherto unimaginable—that is, an actual increase in barbarism in Southeast Asia. What really brought on Watergate remains a mystery. Its fundamental issues grow increasingly uncertain with the passage of time. Despite all the orotund declamations of the episode, it led to no grand reform. There were to be no chastening lessons, no lasting heroes, and no useful myths. All we were left with were dubious platitudes, and they evanesce further with every inescapable revolution of the planet. When it was over, our allies and our enemies were left rubbing their eyes in amazement. Today Watergate looks increasingly like a historic black hole in the national chronicle, and if that is all it turns out to have been we shall be fortunate. Its only benefit is that it brought the retirement of Nixon and with that a quieting of the frantic alarums of the Nixon maniacs.

The publication of RN: *The Memoirs of Richard Nixon* undid even that emaciated benefit. No sooner had its serialization appeared than the Nixon maniacs were howling about enormous profits and moaning that RN contained no lascivious revelations. The bed wetters among them saw the memoirs as the precursor to a political comeback. They mounted a boycott against the book, sold bumper stickers to promote it, and got assurances from their fellows in the book trade that the tome would not be promoted. Some book sellers promised never to sell it. All this is true. Consider the marvel: thousands, perhaps millions, of Americans, the very ones who claim a special relationship with the First Amendment, were now actively engaged in banning a book. Even in exile the man had not lost his touch. I, of course, purchased a copy immediately, and if I had possessed the funds I would have purchased thousands more, gladly sending them to high elected Nixon maniacs with the forged inscription, "Compliments of the Central Intelligence Agency." If my work had landed the book on the best-seller list, so much the better.

The book itself is the usual bouillabaisse of a presidential memoir, considerably better than LBJ's but still a centimeter short of the readable two volumes written by the irrepressible Harry. Some of the writing is crisp and insightful, other passages less so. Every page supports my belief in the essential eeriness of Nixon's career. As the reader proceeds through thirty years of prodigious political dramaturgy, accompanied by this famous narrator, it becomes ever more apparent that there is an odd obliviousness about the man. In every scene, grand or minute, Nixon remains always in the dark about the unearthly powers pulling his strings. Was there something momentous at issue in the Hiss case? Nixon is elliptical. What was the reason for the Cold War? After 1968 he seems to have forgotten. Who were his enemies and why did they hate him? His certitudes go only so far.

Nixon, contrary to the fears of his more obsessive opponents, was a rather ordinary man, distinguished only by his gigantic will to escape ordinariness. Hence he devoted himself to foreign policy. What surer flight from Whittier than to expatiate in the language of power and to ponder the use of power on a global stage? Nixon dreamt immense dreams, and the setting was usually the whole wide world. Even during the grimmest moments of Watergate, times when we had been led to believe he was plotting the overthrow of the Constitution, it now turns out that the poor fish was grandly discoursing to his aides on the Middle East, China's geopolitical interests, Brezhnev's yearnings for a fat and shiny Lincoln. It is an odd twist—and a mark of the inferior men we have elected to the White House—that Nixon was one of our best-equipped presidents for international diplomacy. Yet he blew up, and with his passing, millions of citizens in foreign lands slipped into the claws of Communism and barbarity. Herein lies the saddest part of the Nixon legend. Nixon is gone—hurrah!—but so is any semblance of a serviceable foreign policy.

Nixon was indeed the most reviled man ever to sit in the White House. He was also the easiest laugh in our history. But it is unlikely that Papa Brezhnev ever laughed at him. Ho Chi Minh and General Giap had very little fun at his expense. And as westerners go, Nixon was probably Chou and Mao's only drinking buddy. The final irony of Nixon is that the very qualities that earned him the wary respect of tyrants drove many American liberals right out of their minds. Is it possible that the qualities that made him successful abroad made him a disaster at home? Or was he ever a success anywhere? An indication of the preternatural circumstances surrounding the man is that merely by asking the question one sets off sirens and shouting matches.

17

Nixon As Gatsby:
An Alternative Hypothesis

IF MR. JAY GATSBY of West Egg, Long Island, were alive during the historic impeachment summer of 1974, he would have been making heavy weather of it. Whensoever he motored through the valley of ashes thither into Manhattan, stones would bounce off his roadster, photographers would assail him, and the media "newsteams" would jam microphones into his face. As he passed, fainthearted mothers would call their children indoors. Life would be hard on him, for it was after the image of Gatsby—the man who "paid a high price for living too long with a single dream"—that Richard M. Nixon was sketched. Once again life imitates art; sometimes it makes you want to burn every book in America.

During July of 1974 the Great Nixon sat in his vast white mansion enveloped in desolation. Everything had fallen to pieces, and the dream he had pursued so resolutely and energetically still danced beyond his grasp. The heir to Gatsby had broken up against reality.

Nixon As Gatsby

Nixon could go so far and no farther. His faith in himself, his pragmatism, and his dream just did not provide enough might to overcome Washington's open jaws: subtle conventionalities that he never seemed to grasp, and a one-party political system, the Republican ghost notwithstanding. Perhaps had he been a famous general, a national father figure, he might have triumphed. But he lacked that magic, and so he appealed to the prejudices of the people: their hatred of Communism, their fears for national security.

Nixon did not seem to realize the futility of it all. For a decade the Americano's old certitudes had been beaten out of him; his political wishes had been thwarted by judicial and bureaucratic decrees. Now, in 1974, he had very few prejudices, good or bad, left. He was too intimidated to respond to the old national security tocsin. And so Nixon shouted into an endless night. Every time his Bright Boys tried to spruce up his act they only left him looking all the more ridiculous to the wise and all the more menacing to the Nixon maniacs.

He seems to have been a competent administrator, at least when compared to his doltish successors. But that was not enough. He was in pursuit of an immense delusion, wafting of money, power, and glory. It was his undoing. It was never meant to be.

What Fitzgerald said of the Great Gatsby applied equally to the Great Nixon. They were both in "the service of a vast, vulgar, meretricious beauty." Nixon's service to it was slavish. It forever goaded him into stalking advantages and opportunities. He made people uneasy, and Richard Nixon did not operate well amid uneasy people. In time a madness settled on his house. His aides were the oddest fish to enter the White House until Jimmy and the yokels arrived with their chickens and their Bibles, and Dr. Peter Bourne. Roosevelt hired a brain trust and a lone nudist; Nixon hired bureaucratic psychopaths and sharpsters. He spooked the powers of the town and everyone went into a frenzy, driven by a juvenile American lust for the lurid and the calamitous. When it all ended it was the nation's Bicentennial and we elected a president possessed of all the creepiness of the Good Woodrow and none of his intelligence.

It is true that all the elements of Nixon's dream did not spring full-blown from his own imagination. The conceptions of power, of politics, of virtue, and of money were derivative: part Kennedy, part Roosevelt, part Hollywood, part Manhattan. It was old stuff. But, like Gatsby, Nixon was the rare man who dared to dream of it all at once.

The rootless pragmatism of Nixon had once guided Gatsby. They shared the same dubious taste. No matter how much optimism they brought to their respective visions, they were doomed. They were doomed, I suspect, because one cannot pursue preposterous dreams at the expense of reality forever. And they were doomed because the world will yield only so much to cleverness, audacity, and obsessive self-interest.

18

Mike Gravel: The Future of American Statecraft

IN THE very early 1970s, before General Giap brought peace and freedom to Vietnam, terrible fevers were on America. A senseless war was being waged in Southeast Asia by Americans wedded to what the profs jauntily disparaged as "the long-discredited domino theory." Local police, the CIA, and the FBI were having things pretty much their own way with thousands of idealistic black militants and college protesters, despite remonstrances from Dr. Noam Chomsky, Dr. Jane Fonda, and a handful of other conscientious observers who dared utter what is now conventional wisdom: America was becoming a police state. And back at the hearth, middle-class Americans were sullenly staring into their TVs, coldly acceding to the diabolical Nixon, and donning the American flag. No wonder the *New York Review of Books* had printed page one instructions for making a Molotov cocktail. These were hazardous times. One had to be prepared to protect one-self on a moment's notice, and you would not expect a good liberal to resort to handguns. That would be playing right into the paws of the National Rifle Association.

During those grim times George McGovern and I were of the same mind in that we believed that what America needed most was a laugh. My opportunities for comedy were limited, but McGoo was better placed. He spent most of 1972 criss-crossing the country, selflessly restoring the horselaugh to its former eminence. The campaign elicited many ho-ho-hos and almost as many votes, but in the end McGoo lost, a tragic victim of the schemes of E. Howard Hunt, Gordon Liddy, and, of course, the crafty Nixon. Once again Americans were wincing their way through the evening news. There was the painful experience of Watergate, an economic swoon, Nixon's shabby exit, and the Machiavellian pardon. Ford merely continued the hell, causing me to conclude that never again must America have a Republican as president. It is simply unfair to the liberals. It frightens them.

Moreover, Republicans are provocative. Twice in 1975 Mr. Ford provoked members of the constituency of conscience to do him in. The *New York Times* tried to be helpful, declaring in the fall of that year that it was no longer advisable for the President to leave the White House, certainly not if he intended to go to California. But it was no use. Ford would not stay put, and the nation grew grimmer. Morale sank to its lowest level since the Depression, and there it remained for months. News that Richard Nixon was again playing golf, writing his memoirs, and planning further personal contributions to the commonweal only added anxiety to the drear. Something had to be done to bring back the smiling, enthusiastic Yank of yesteryear. Once again America needed to laugh.

The project was too vast for the private sector. It cried out for federal intervention and fortunately the amusing potential of the public sector had become manifest, viz.: the Postal Service, Medicare, the contents of the *Congressional Record*, the presidential campaigns, etc. Actually various pols were already revving up for the 1976 presidential contest. There was the Rt. Hon. Milton Shapp, head of a state government long one of the most corrupt in the Union, and running on a dainty platform of goody-goody liberalism, the pro-people/anti-big business variety. There was the Rt. Hon. Fred Harris, solemnly promising to invite those who supported him down to the White House for an overnight stay once the requisite act of God had been effected and he had become president. There was Jimmy Carter from Georgia, and there was Stanley Arnold from New York. All were clownish, but unfortunately none was reliably clownish. The problem was that none had promoted himself as an avowed clown, and America needed clowns who were in earnest. Besides, to laugh at politicians sincerely running for our nation's highest office would be disrespectful. What I had in mind was a new kind of presidential campaign populated with a new kind of candidate, a forthright, single-minded clown dedicated to the public interest.

Agreed, in the past we occasionally raised clowns to the White House, but always to our surprise and often to the surprise of the president-elect. The ensuing amusement often came at the expense of our patriotism and in time gave way to sadness. Harding was, surely, a clown, but few Americans realized this, even when he was launching those tortured orotundities from his Marion, Ohio, front porch. During his early years in office he was full of high purpose and playing the presidential game with great assiduity. But then at midterm he paused, he heard chortles from the sidelines, his friends were playing him the fool. The thing was too much. He went to San Francisco and died, a clown with a broken heart. There is nothing in this tale to gladden the spirit.

Public Nuisances

How different it would be with an admitted clown. An admitted clown would feel no embarrassment as the guffaws rolled in. To the contrary, he would feel the flush of accomplishment and strive to new heights—perhaps a toney uniform for the president, perhaps for the White House staff roller skates to speed up the governmental process, maybe even an energy program that is the moral equivalent of war. Never again would voters suffer indecision over the propriety of laughing aloud at the State of the Union message. They would not feel stunned or indignant with presidential pratfalls. They could roar with laughter the minute the election returns were in. They could laugh unashamedly right down to their leader's last gaffe, and their leader could laugh with them. The old American ebullience would revive. George McGovern would be redeemed.

Looking for a self-professed clown to boom for the presidency was not an easy task, even on the eve of our Bicentennial. American politicians take themselves very seriously, despite the nuthouse aura surrounding them. For a while I considered Senator Lowell Weicker of the great state of Connecticut. His penchant for calling press conferences wherein he would variously bawl and holler was amusing, but it turned out that he did not return my calls. Senator Charles Mathias was a possibility. He was then raising chickens in his office, but before I could raise the subject, I hit upon the perfect clown, a man born to lift America from the mulligrubs then and forever. He had already shown a yearning for higher office, and at the first sign of interest in his presidential campaign it was apparent he would be off, running, and perfectly willing to make a fool of himself.

My candidate was a senator already well versed in national politics. Back in 1972 he had actually run for the *vice-*presidency. To a chorus of hoots and laughter he had com-

mandeered the podium at that year's Democratic Convention
and violently seconded himself. It was one of the most asinine
speeches ever heard on prime-time national television. My
1976 candidate was a proud proponent of acupuncture and the
first senator ever to place his noble body under the acupunc-
turist's mysterious needles. Further, he was a visionary. He
was the Senate's staunchest supporter of transcendental meditation, having fathered Senate Resolution 64 "to increase public awareness of transcendental meditation" and to make the
second week of November "World Plan Week—U.S.A." He
was forty-five years old, a member of the Unitarian-
Universalist Church, and a failed trailer-camp magnate, who,
when he married, had taken Miss Fur Rendezvous of 1958 for
his lawful wedded wife.

He was a certified liberal, an advocate of peace, and—except for his marriage to Miss Fur Rendezvous of 1958—he was
in good odor with environmentalists. He was also a man of
compassion and inner strength whose imaginative conscience
made him an instant celebrity when, on the evening of June
29, 1971, he summoned the press to the Capitol where he
blubbered through a public reading of the purloined Pentagon
Papers. Tears streaking down his handsome face, he would
pause occasionally to exclaim and to shriek to a tiny audience
composed of agape newsmen and one mesmerized congressman. Furthermore this historic piece of *Realpolitik* went on in
the chamber of the Senate Subcommittee on Capitol Buildings and Grounds. My candidate had chosen that room himself! When, at 1:00 A.M., he admitted to being "physically incapable of continuing any longer," his uneasy aides rushed
him from the scene as though he were a dead fish left too long
in the sun. There was my candidate, and if I could just identify that congressman who sat up listening to his soap opera I
would have my vice-presidential candidate.

Public Nuisances

The senator's aides were obviously humorless, and I did not ingratiate myself with them when I suggested their boss, Senator Maurice Robert (Mike) Gravel—as if you were still in the dark—for the presidency. Nonetheless, I thought Senator Gravel was at that time the American pol most likely to make America laugh and I did everything I could to boom his candidacy in the pages of *The American Spectator*. Yet the campaign never took wing, and six weeks into the presidency of Jimmy Carter, I, of course, had to admit that I had been in error.

19

Jimmy: The Wonderboy

IN AN EARLIER ERA Jimmy Carter of Plains, Georgia, would be devoting himself to procuring his young daughter's first pair of shoes, a bottle of Peruna for a fat wife, and a dusty flivver for himself. At day's end he would withdraw to the humid coziness of the local Coca-Cola parlor, there to discourse upon the latest intrigues of the Popish camorra and to remain *au courant* with reports of frightening suicide rates experienced by misguided Negroes lured to the Sodoms of the North and taught to read. As the years ambled on, and his wife fattened, he would feel the itch of public service. He would compose diatribes about Demon Rum or the abominations committed by hyphenates swarming into New York City. Folks would take note, and—if he were as gifted as he is now—one day he would hit pay dirt with a speech identifying Jesus Christ as the first Elk and be raised up to high public office. Eventually, he might even buy a judgeship from local Prohibitionists and so, midst the dust and the peanut vines, age in dignity until felled by a necrotic liver. All in all, a better Jimmy Carter, one more intellectual, more principled, intrinsically more interesting, and far less menacing to the Republic.

Yet Jimmy Carter was not given a historic role in the America of the 1920s; rather his role came in the 1970s, thirty years into the palmiest era of economic growth known to man. Materially he longs for very little. In his lifetime he has seen the wizardry of indoor plumbing come to his Plains, Georgia, manse. The streets are paved, flivvers abound, the hookworm has been outwitted, and electric-powered gadgetry eases his worldly woes. The Pope's siege has been lifted, and all those rascals who denied him the fellowship of his black brethren are today but an inscrutable memory. Progress has invaded Plains, and with it has come the modern American system of values, a system esteeming wealth and bustle and power, at least when that wealth and power are amassed by those who pontificate against wealth and power. The old Southern values were a tragedy. They have been replaced by a farce.

In 1965 Jimmy was at one with thousands of other middle-aged American men: rich, saucy, ignorant, and bored. He had energetically thrown himself into making it; but once he made it, life lost its old lilt. The days became dull burdens. He took up square dancing, but it edified him not at all. He sought renewal in the stock cars, but the exhaust fumes gave him nausea. Biographers tell us Jimmy and his wife even sought refuge from their existential travail in Americus, Georgia, where bowling alleys were plentiful, but the cosmic questions still swelled up, begging to be answered.

Finally there was that historic reunion with his sister, Ruth Carter Stapleton, wherein she explained the idiotic smile then continually disfiguring her face, causing dark speculations amongst the local Pharisees, and alarming her family. According to Ruth, she had drunk of the Blood of the Lamb and become a Bible-pounding evangelist learned in the ways of su-

pernatural chiropractorship. The revelation was to be taken
seriously, for she was no primitive. She had taken thirty hours
of psychology up at the state university, so Jimmy listened.
Ruth urged him to accept Christ into his heart. He felt a heavenly intruder and shortly thereafter became the peppiest species of Christian. He took up politics with renewed energy.
And with these two mighty heaves Jimmy illustrated that the
Founders knew what they were about when they remonstrated
against the mingling of Church and State. Something there is
about the spiritual and the political that summons forth the
petty tyrant and gives him large opportunities to work his philistine will upon his fellows. No pol since William Jennings
Bryan had thrown both Holy Writ and Democracy into an assault on the citizenry. But when Sister Ruth elucidated her
secret to Brother Jimmy, he saw its possibilities at once; the
Wonderboy's scramble for power had begun, and it was to be
astonishingly swift.

Happily, the Great Emancipator had been a Republican, so
when Jimmy chose his party the choice was both effortless and
auspicious. He was to be a Democrat. Such is the colossal
good luck that seems to have hovered about him from the
moment he forsook the bowling temples of Americus and
took up public service. In 1966 he launched a preposterous
campaign for the governorship of Georgia and was so easily de-
feated that a candidate less blessed by the good fairy would
have been esteemed for life as a laughingstock never to be
taken seriously again. Yet, four years later, the grinning dunce
of 1966 was again tramping through the Georgia back country;
only this time everyone knew his name, and he had the endorsement of such worthies as the Honorable Lester Maddox
and of such respected citizens' groups as the Georgia Ku Klux
Klan. Even when he honeyfogled the most exalted strata of
Georgian society, luck covered for him. Solemnly he would

declare himself "basically a redneck," and no one in the audience would let out a hoot or pause to question him about the five-million-dollar Carter fortune. He was a child of felicity.

Once in the governor's mansion, his time was essentially his own; for the trickier questions of governing Georgia were then being handled by the federal courts. Jimmy had time to indulge his darker side by bickering with the state legislature and impersonating various Old Testament eminences. More importantly, however, he was able to assume ambiguous responsibility for governmental acts, while the courts did the dirty work. Ambiguity is today the essence of Carterism. Pretending helplessness in the face of a despotic judicial system, he has suavely assumed both sides of vexed issues like abortion and busing, apparently to the complacent satisfaction of large numbers of voters. Such blatant dissimulations were rarely practiced so successfully before Jimmy rose up from the Georgian boondocks, but he had the good fortune to hold office in one of the first states governed by *mandamus*, and he quickly learned the usefulness of this democratic innovation. As judicial tyranny overtakes the federal government doubtless many elected officials will emulate the Wonderboy's technique, but history will duly record that this was his discovery, a discovery made possible mainly by his fortunate origins.

In 1974 Jimmy kissed his mother on the cheek and struck out for the 1976 Democratic nomination. His luck remained golden, for in 1976—as in 1972—all the major Democratic contenders had again forgotten to study the abstruse nominating procedures of their party. Jimmy had studied them for months, and halfway through the primaries he was being touted as a political genius. Truth to tell, he harvests very few pearls from his noodle, and he made a pathetic spectacle of himself on numerous occasions; but his competitors were unhorsed by their own party's reform mania, and Jimmy—

unblack, unyoung, and unfeminine—was sole beneficiary. After the convention all he faced was the GOP, a party that had been decapitated, was bleeding profusely, and had lost all sense of purpose. No pol in this century has been so favored by sheer luck as Jimmy; it is a matter that surely has not escaped the notice of Sister Ruth.

Yet few pols have ever been more banal, more tedious, and more stupendously uninteresting. Perhaps had Jimmy not so recently and thoroughly been deKluxed and debumpkinized there might be more to him. He might not be the near vacuum who now leaves almost every writer maundering. Yet modernity overwhelmed Plains, and Jimmy has been sanitized. Search the record, you will find not one diverting anecdote, nor one piquant quality in this essentially vacant man. He is all go-getter, goody-goody, and speed reading. LBJ was a cauldron of passions, Henry Kissinger would break from diplomacy to visit the *Jeu de Paume,* even the hellish Nixon battered Chopin on his piano. Notifications that Jimmy immerses himself in Niebuhr, Wagner, and Dylan Thomas are so much claptrap. He has no more capacity for the higher intellection than for baking soufflés. The essential Jimmy is the automaton who crisscrosses America serving up his Laodicean banalities in a set discourse that is unique to all American political rhetoric for its utterly shameless flattery. Though he was hailed as the political marvel of the hour, not one pol has aped his appallingly insipid sermonic. By the fall of 1978, a mere two years after his nomination, no serious Democratic candidate in the land was seeking his endorsement. Even an American politician has his limits.

That this philistine became the candidate espoused by the *New York Review of Books* and promoted by all modern sophisticates is the most amusing spectacle since the Catholics discovered JFK's randiness. But the spectacle of it also illuminates the barrenness of our era. Think of it! The morality-and-enlightenment claque, the fastidious moralists who banished Nixon, settled for a second-generation Babbitt, dismissing from their consciences the blatancy of his fibs and the tedious philistinism of his hollow character. If ever one needed evidence that mere power is the moderns' only serious value, their endorsement of the Wonderboy provides evidence in profusion. Power to gratify a ravenous and ridiculous ego is the moderns' most holy sacrament, indeed their only one. So they held their noses and spouted for Jimmy. A mere two years after Nixon the Democrats actually nominated a Nixon of their own. Jimmy is a ruthless, relentless pursuer of power; and that is the whole of him. Agreed, it is revolting to listen to that limp, desiccated rhetoric and to witness his bald position-taking, but it was amusing to observe such moderns as Norman Mailer as they fabricated from mere nothingness an "interesting," "decent," "pleasant" man, a Protestant JFK. And it was even more amusing to see the moderns desert him in hysteria when it became apparent that he was the most ill-equipped man to inhabit the White House in this century.

All this was clear in the fall of 1976, and I endured much opprobrium when I then said as much in *The American Spectator*. For months thereafter pundits would sidle up to me and upbraid me for doubting the Wonderboy's brilliance. Yet in time my critics fell silent, and two years later when I was reflecting on Jimmy's character for this book I found that my original estimate printed two years ago stood up so well that there was no reason not to reprint it here with only the scantiest changes and no retractions. Jimmy was that obvious! What prevented others from recognizing this sad detail?

20

Jimmy: Midway in the Revels

THE SAGA BEGAN on January 20, 1977, the date on which Jimmy was inaugurated 39th President. His inaugural address, intoned in his famous *andante con ping pong* cadence, was an arrestingly straightforward and simple-witted oration that should have answered immediately and forever his campaign's famed rhetorical question: "Why Not the Best?" Why not indeed! The Wonderboy had entered the presidency with exactly six years' experience in Georgia state government behind him. When he was inaugurated, the current edition of *Who's Who* still listed his profession as "farmer and warehouseman." Thirteen days after this soporific monologue he delivered his first "Fireside Chat," the substantive highlight of which was his request that citizens restrain themselves from sending him "gifts." About that time there appeared the first pictures of our President tripping Ford-like in front of the White House. It was an impressive beginning, but for the first few months not many caught on. Except for the hijinks of the

Rev. Young and the scalping of one or two of Jimmy's more maladroit appointments, Washington remained in a protracted and blissful coma.

This was to be expected. Our sudden release from the Ford fascism was bound to gladden many a Washington heart, and a temporary relaxation in our indigenous freedom fighters' eternal vigilance was only natural. More importantly, however, it is in the early months of an administration that the president presents his policies and that the pundits and pols politely scrutinize them. It is a quiet time. In Mr. Carter's case, it was an especially quiet time, for he did not seem to have many policies or even many ideas about policies. What policies he did have amounted to sheer tedium—the Great Society as understood by Dinah Shore and implemented by George McGovern with assistance from the Plains, Georgia, Rotary. Harding drunk was better equipped for the presidency than Jimmy, though here it ought to be recorded that when the voice of the people was heard in 1976, the voice was faint: 27.5 percent of the people said Jimmy, 26 percent said Jerry, and a whopping 46.5 percent said yech. So the pundits remained quiescent, but by autumn the average American began to shift in his seat. Soon even the pundits began to stir. Andy Young, Bert Lance, Rosalynn, Amy, Miss Lillian. Zounds!

It was in early November, 1977, not yet a year into the Populist Era, that the president's coterie of yokels was roused from reveries on the perfect *filet de catfish* by the shouts of the pollsters. Jimmy's popularity had mysteriously evaporated. Holy shee-it! At the White House, Ham and Jody, our president's dungareed aides, hurriedly removed their socks from the radiator, thrust their hooves into their clodhoppers, and with shirttails flapping galloped into the Oval Office. The Yankees had done woke up! Congress was in mutiny! The conservatives were mad and the liberals were madder. Even the Washington press corps no longer saw the charm of having a pack of Snopeses listening to *Scheherazade* in the White House's West Wing.

The yokels' holiday in the big city was over. Something stupendous needed to be done or it was back to the all-night Standard station. Fortunately for the boys, Jimmy had hired a Yankee pollster, Patrick Caddell, who had already devised a political strategy memorandum to ensure Jimmy's victory in 1980. We know this because the astonishing document was leaked to the *New York Times*. According to Caddell, "Too many good people have been beaten because they tried to substitute substance for style." Of course, Jimmy was in no danger of perishing from a superabundance of substance, and when Ham and Jody heard of Caddell's prescription for presidential greatness they came alive with enthusiasm. Very simply, Caddell prescribed a "continuing political campaign." That day there resounded from the Oval Office many "hot damns" and "taaarnations." It was a day for jubilation. The boys would not return home in 1980! The people could be hornswoggled once again! During the next month our president showed the old fire of Campaign '76. First he went a-ridin' through the slums of the South Bronx to condole with the victims of Wall Street. Then he laced up his own clodhoppers, charged onto the White House lawn, and put on the feed bag with "the Peanut Brigade," 500 credulous Georgians who had staffed his 1976 campaign and with whom he would occasionally visit to illustrate some obscure point in the populist whim-wham. "These are my closest friends in all the world," he sighed, and the press quoted him. "We're part of the same family," he purred. "I'm a redneck just like you."

A certain breed of low-grade American seems to fall for this drivel, and Jimmy and the boys knew it. When in trouble he would mix such sentimental flummeries with outraged denunciations of lawyers, doctors, businessmen, automobile mechanics, almost anyone who produced anything, almost anyone footing the bill for our government's good works. At times his philippics would be so violent that they would astonish even the Gucci Bolsheviks of Georgetown.

But brazen flattery, unctuous maundering, and objurgations of the tax-paying public availed him naught. Moreover, the polls continued to sink him. In a fever, he began traveling to foreign lands, whether invited or not. In late December 1977 he went on a historic nine-day, seven-nation tour that was as comic as it was useless. In Poland his arrival speech will be remembered as the most hilarious ever delivered by an American president on foreign soil. Aided by a spectacularly inept translator, Jimmy was seen to be gravely notifying an assemblage of shocked Polish dignitaries that he had abandoned America forever. Apropos of human rights, he was heard to assure the Poles that he understood all the sexual yearnings of the Polish people. Chortles commenced, yet onward he lunged, piling malapropism atop malapropism. Distractedly he would look up from his prepared text and discover his audience convulsed in laughter, yet on he would trudge, amusing them all the more and assuring his place as the most thundering hind ever to bloviate in the land of the kielbasa. Did he ever ask any of his aides what the guffawing was all about? Who knows, and who knows how many of his aides would know. On his right stood Jordan and to his left stood Powell, both loyally shouldering his perplexity, at least until the Warsaw saloons opened.

From Poland the boys went to Teheran, where Jimmy attended the Shah's New Year's Eve party, took aboard two glasses of wine, and turned weepy. In India he astonished government officials by growing dyspeptic when they temporarily resisted taking him and his photographers to an impoverished village. During a state dinner, he, and only he, was harassed by a common housefly, thus necessitating the professional services of Prime Minister Desai's official Hindu fly swattist. And during the meal he whispered contemptuous remarks about Desai while facing a mysterious electronic device that, upon further inspection, turned out to be a microphone. Alas, the infernal contraption was full of juice, and the Wonderboy's discourtesies were broadcast all over the dining room. In Paris he enlivened a critically important national election by embracing a radical party leader and notifying him of their shared *metaphysique*. The Paris stock market tumbled 2.5 percent and the astounded leader of France's center-right government began to sweat.

By the time the Wonderboy returned home, the whole world had grown interested in the political science of our populist genius. In foreign chancelleries everywhere, diplomats would crowd before their teletypes, eager for every fresh report from Washington. Not since the Marshall Plan had Washington attracted such avid curiosity abroad. Even in remote Bangladesh there must have resided a lowly peasant who, after plodding through furrows, his face impassively set toward the undulating hindquarters of a mortgaged bovine, would rush home to inquire: "What's the latest with the Washington yokel, eh?" Such an inquiry would rarely leave him unconsoled.

There was the time during Middle East negotiations when he threw the Arab world into an instantaneous tumult by doltishly misstating his government's policy *vis-à-vis* Jerusalem, which he referred to as the capital of Israel. There was the time he greeted the President of Romania with the wrong national anthem, and there was his curious appearance at an economic summit in England during the spring of 1977. Practically

166

every economy in the West was having difficulty, and what was it that most concerned Jimmy? That the poet Dylan Thomas had yet to be commemorated in Westminster Abbey's Poets' Corner. The matter absorbed him.

The leaders of all the other countries were addressing themselves to such worries as inflation and unemployment, but not the Wonderboy. Instead, he went off and sought out the Abbey's archdeacon, informing him of his desire to "personally recommend" the Welsh rummy for the Poets' Corner. The move was met by an embarrassed silence, and, as Prime Minister Callaghan tried to engage the attention of the leader of the free world in the problem of his balance of payments, Jimmy hit upon a new approach. He promised the archdeacon to "pray for his soul if you'll memorialize him." Still no luck, and as the summit went on, Jimmy announced his intention to take his crusade to the South Wales fishing village where Mr. Thomas is interred and where Scotch fumes still rise from his grave. Only Mr. Callaghan's exasperated warnings that the president's arrival there might ignite demonstrations among Welsh nationalists dissuaded our president.

Doubtless everyone has his own treasured memory of a Carter botch. My own favorite was a flag-raising ceremony in Spokane, Washington. There, the smartest young man ever to cast his shadow in Plains, Georgia, could not find the American flag, though there was not a drunk in the crowd who shared his difficulty. Sternly he stood, hand on heart, staring stonily into the faces of a thousand Spokanese as they gazed upon Old Glory rising majestically behind him. Did our president take the hint and amiably turn around? Not at all. The lone populist stared resolutely forward, and it was not until a local pol gently remonstrated with him that he gave up his hilarious pose. It must have been an unusually quiet flight back to Washington, and my guess is that no sooner had Jimmy returned to the White House than he had Ham Jordan on the telephone hollering at the aforementioned Spokanese pol and threatening him with every sort of horror.

Ham was the Wonderboy's chief assistant president, and as the late Niccolo Machiavelli was wont to advise, first impressions of a ruler and of his intelligence are gained from seeing the men he has around him. Ham was never far, and he was almost always a slob in trouble, yet Jimmy stood by him. He stood by him with such doltish devotion that old Niccolo would not have scratched his noodle for long before delivering up a judgment on the political wizard of Campaign '76.

Ham's problems were always of an arrestingly ribald nature. There was the time he was caught *flagrante delicto* with his paw on the *pectoralis major* of Mrs. Amal Ghorbal, lawful wedded wife of the ambassador from the sovereign state of Egypt. During this crisis the White House pothered indignantly and indecisively, at first issuing denials and then piously requesting to see the smoking gun, so to speak. The Wonderboy handled Ham's next adventure more presidentially. When the news appeared in the *Washington Post* that Ham had tried to charm a local beauty in Sarsfield's saloon by spitting Amaretto and cream down her bosom, the White House responded with a 33-page white paper. For once the kabosh had been firmly placed on the merchants of scandal. This document, possibly the most important paper of the entire Carter administration, has practically every ingredient of the Carter genius. It is thorough, solemn, shifty, inane, ludicrous.

Fashioned by White House lawyers, the 8,ooo-word, tightly reasoned brief takes us right to the scene of the atrocity, querying Sarsfield's surprisingly eloquent mixologist, Mr. Daniel V. Marshall III. From Mr. Marshall's testimony alone it becomes clear for all who would see that poor Ham was the victim of his own gallantry. Apparently he was unwinding after a day of statecraft. Quietly quaffing his interesting drink in an inconspicuous stall, our president's likable factotum would occasionally jollify the saloon's ambience with a genial belch but nothing more. Suddenly a bevy of cuties fell upon him. As Mr. Marshall recreated the scene: "Girls were coming up to Hamilton and woo-woo. You know what I mean?" Naturally Ham shrank back in disgust, and "did something to the point where enough's enough. I think one of the girls got insulted." Yet there was no spitting: "That would have been quite a mess, and she certainly wasn't wet." There you have it.

Ham was only the most newsworthy of the Wonderboy's aides. There were others: press secretary Jody Powell, who had been ejected from the Air Force Academy for cheating on a history examination; presidential drug advisor Dr. Peter Bourne, forced to resign when caught issuing bogus prescriptions for controlled drugs; and so forth. Two years into the Carter administration, it became apparent that America was being governed by a concatenation of jokes. The horselaugh had replaced our national anthem. Dogberries were on sale in vending machines in the White House and in souvenir shops all over Washington. The economy was in ominous condition. Jimmy's legislative proposals were irrelevant. The Congress was more mutinous than ever, and Jimmy's foreign policy continued to astound the world. It combined abusive denunciations of the Soviets with unilateral disarmament. Steadily a pervasive sense of unease began to spread. Republicans and Democrats restrained their laughter and even their criticisms as they saw the Wonderboy grow in puniness with every passing day. Western security no longer seemed dependent on American power but on the "bonkers factor," to wit:

the perception that America was governed by a real nut and that there was no telling what he might do when aroused. The Soviets were edgy; NATO leaders were even edgier.

August 1978 will be remembered by historians as the catastasis of the Wonderboy's Populist Era. It was then that the White House yokels and their antagonists began asking fundamental questions about political conditions. The yokels began their reassessment right after poor Ham was assaulted while at a Georgetown *soirée* by an unidentified guest wielding a chocolate mousse, that expensive French dessert that had just become all the rage with the Georgia mafia. After being introduced to the delicacy sometime earlier in the year, the boys grew to love it, and no longer were they so distressed when Georgetown hostesses refused to serve them Moon Pies and Dr. Pepper. Yet when Ham got walloped, and the boys saw what the Gallic potion could do to a double-knit leisure suit, a chill went through the White House. The boys began to wonder if life in Washington was really worth it. Henceforth Georgetown was looked upon with fear, and it was a rare Carter aide who would go near a chocolate mousse. (As one unidentified aide remarked, "Ah'd sooner kiss a pig thun tech one of them thengs.") Morale within the White House was at its nadir, and many of the boys began to yearn for the reassuring sounds of home sweet home: of gentle cows lowing in the front yard, of horseflies struggling to free themselves from flypaper strips, of granddaddy hitting the spittoon from a dozen paces.

The questions from outside the White House grew more serious too. August 5, 1978, was the date from which a deeper, more pessimistic questioning of the Carter administration began. On that day Senator Barry Goldwater uttered the heretofore unutterable. Speaking in Chattanooga, Tennessee, he stated his belief that the Wonderboy was, indeed, an idiot. It was a decidedly reckless statement, for anyone with any knowledge at all knows that an idiot is a mentally defective person with an intelligence quotient of less than 25. President Carter had graduated from the Naval Academy, he was a former governor of the largest state east of the Mississippi River, and he was the devoted husband of Rosalynn Carter, known and reverenced throughout Washington as "the steel magnolia." Jimmy was *not* an idiot, yet Goldwater's declaration did set minds to musing. If not an idiot, what about an imbecile? Perhaps a moron?

After two years as President of the United States Jimmy still speaks glowingly of eliminating the three-martini lunch (known as the fifty-dollar martini lunch during Campaign '76), filthy or deceitful language in public life, and strong spirits at White House dinners. What is more, as he informed North Carolina tobacco growers on two occasions in the summer of 1978, his administration is dedicated to making "the smoking of tobacco even more safe." Are these the policies of an idiot? Not at all; these are policies that demand vigorous staff work, and every day the achievement of the Carter staff becomes ever more manifest. Ham, Jody, and Dr. Bourne were only three of the Wonderboy's appointees. There were others. There was Jerry Rafshoon, the Rev. Andrew Young, Cousin Hugh Carter, Bert Lance, and Miss Midge Costanza, the spunky Rochester, New York, intellectual who gained distinction for sending Mr. Carter memos suggesting such large thoughts as that White House staff members be required to make visits to the Lincoln or Jefferson memorials.

This last idea came to Miss Costanza after she had sought to "reenergize" herself during her own visitation to the Jefferson Memorial at 4:00 A.M. According to the *Washington Post*, Miss Costanza, whose special responsibility for minorities had earned her the unspoken title of White House Minister to the

Public Nuisances

Kooks, remarked: "Every time I came across 'man' or 'men' I changed it mentally. I said, 'IT WAS PERSON, TOM, IT WAS PERSON! OKAY, TOM. ISN'T IT IRONIC THAT IT TOOK A WOMAN TO BE REENERGIZED RIGHT HERE?' " More ironic still is the fact that but a few short weeks after this reenergizing orgy, Miss Costanza resigned. Perhaps she left to write a monograph on Jefferson; as she herself had observed: "He was so brilliant. And yet he wasn't fully informed." Being "informed" was an obsession with Jimmy and his staff. Never before had such a group inhabited our federal government—and Senator Goldwater called Jimmy an idiot!

I deny that Jimmy Carter is an idiot or any other variety of mental defective. Rather he is the perfect representative of New Age Egalitarianism. His politics reveal the vagaries of a really cheap mind. He has no ideas and no ideals worthy of scrutiny. His vision is that of a small-town boomer dreaming of a paved road for Main Street. His philosophy is a stew of jealousy, superstition, and banality. He is without dignity. If ever he were to be impeached, my guess is that, after a review of his policies and locutions, he would be acquitted by reason of inanity. Yet Mr. Carter is the only president we have, and it is the duty of all Americans to close ranks behind him, or better still, in front of him, and not let the world see what 27.5 percent of the adult population of this country did to us.

21

Walter Mondale:
The Goody-Goody Ethos

December it was, 1964, when the most winning young man ever to inspect peas in Elmore, Minnesota, arrived in the United States Senate, not by election but by investiture. Lucky Walter "Fritz" Mondale had been Vice-President Hubert Humphrey's earnest factotum since the late 1940s, and it is a venerable rule of America's political science that when politics does not reward the congenital malcontent it rewards the dutiful.

Mondale's maiden Senate speech laid bare the problem of world hunger, and that things have yet to improve is no reflection on his commitment. The vehemence of the thing was awesome. After his many shouts and an occasional leap into the air, it was apparent for all to see that young Mondale was already one of the most promising voices of goody-goodyism on the entire Washington scene. True to Hubert Humphrey's predictions, "Fritz" was going to be a wow. Yet notwithstanding his ardor and the many constructive suggestions he made that day, hunger persists; only the grandiloquent speeches and the governmental agencies have fattened. It is the kind of dispiriting news that makes it very hard to remain sanguine about the system. Yet Fritz has slogged on, gamely offering the liberals' statist elixir and never giving himself over to street demonstrations or pipe bombs.

Here was a prodigy—even in progressive and idealistic Minnesota. Neither the Green Giant Company nor greater Elmore will ever see his like again, and bear in mind that Elmore is a hotbed of cheery, busybody Methodism. In his youth Mondale was positive, prompt, upright, ingratiating, and slippery. He has never changed, nor—if I read him correctly—does he think America has changed. To him everything is just as Upton Sinclair discovered it in 1906.

For over a dozen years Mondale whirred along in the United States Senate, becoming in time that body's Great Solemnizer. Nothing he touched was ever commonplace. For him it was always the Eroica in E-flat major; and if from the orchestra there occasionally sounded the strangled gurgle of a Methodist moralizer, his audiences failed to object.

Mondale is a man of stunning charm. It is his custom to fix his stare on those with whom he converses and to focus his eyes and set his jaw so as to suggest "I care about you, personally." Whether this is a studied mannerism or the manifestation of some optical defect remains unknown, but it is a cold fish who leaves Mondale's presence unmoved.

One of the sad consequences of Mondale's mastery over those whom he accosts is that journalistic accounts of him constitute a tedious procession of repetitious anecdotes amplifying his high moral character, his intelligence, and his Boy Scouts of America demeanor. Nothing informative or even plausible about the man beneath the halo ever extrudes from the press. Does he take a nip? Just two in an evening. Does he admire a well-turned ankle? Only in the Christian context. Does he go in for crank calls, massage parlors, or any of the other leisure-time activities now so popular with our elected officials? It is unchronicled. The blandness of my colleagues' accounts leaves me with the suspicion that Mondale's stupefying goody-goodyism poses a greater threat to freedom of the press than did Richard Milhous Nixon at the height of his despotic power.

After poring over the published accounts of the man's life, about all we know for sure is that over the years the Great Solemnizer has stood up against child abuse, consumer fraud, drug misuse, presidential perfidy, and reckless driving—this despite the enormous risks such controversial positions entail. Sedulously and intrepidly he has spoken out for civil rights, families, the powerless, quality education, decency, and meat inspection, even as powerful opposition rose up to destroy him. Doubtless these courageous stands have placed his life in mortal danger many times. There must have been nights when his aides would not let him go home alone. His laundry was done personally by Joan, his loving wife and somewhat of an intellectual in her own right. When Mondale joined the Carter administration as number 2 yokel Joan was made the White House's special potentate on The Arts, becoming a kind of populist equivalent of Lorenzo the Magnificent. At any rate Mondale has, through all the controversies and perils, remained steadfast to postindustrial Puritanism, namely a working relationship with God for the extirpation of other people's sinfulness, personal salvation through good intentions, good public relations, good government, and the taxing power.

The child abusers fought back. Cunning lobbyists were employed. The drug pushers organized and reviled him in their publications. The powerful stayed up nights plotting his downfall. There were tense moments whenever he showed up at the

Public Nuisances

establishments of Emilio Pucci and Aldo Gucci, but what was he to do? One cannot go naked on this orb. The man from Elmore would face down the running dogs of capitalism and buy a new tie, spending on it as much as some Americanoes spend on a pair of shoes. Remember, Joan was an aesthete. Was he to wear ties from Sears Roebuck and break up his marriage? But I move too rapidly. Let us return to the man and his works.

From his puppyhood at the hearth of an itinerant Methodist preacher and Democratic Farmer-Labor fanatic, through his college days—interrupted by a mission to Washington as first leader of the student arm of the Americans for Democratic Action—he has dedicated his life to what he himself calls "the politics of human need." Yet he is not to be put down as an ideologue or a dogmatist, for he has loudly disavowed both crutches. His mind is undarkened by the least vestige of prejudice. He lives by pure reason and a good heart. With remarkable candor he declares himself to be a simple "problem-solver," a kind of public utility in human form. While attempting to charm his way to the 1976 Democratic presidential nomination he went even so far as to describe himself as a "problem-oriented, pragmatic liberal." Let the chips fall where they may.

Now, when Mondale insists that he has never fallen into the clutches of ideology some will grow skeptical. The ADA's first youth leader was no ideologue? What of his consistently left-liberal voting record, his slavish devotion to left-liberal passions, and that historic day in the early seventies when the unctuous senator from Minnesota found himself in the odd position of voting against prayer in public schools while managing a floor fight for an avant-garde pornography report, which was itself so scabrous that it had sent every senator on the Hill into hiding? A memorable day's work, that: the problem-oriented, pragmatic liberal thwarts prayer, promotes

porn, and denies through it all any reliance whatsoever on ideology. Then, too, some will rebel at the pundits' insistence that he is so sweet, compassionate, decent—in the words of the *New Republic*, "a man of human feeling." After all, he obviously relished his service as Carter's hatchet man. With gusto he would tie the hapless Jerry to every calamity from Watergate back to the great Florida land boom, and he showed no compunction about letting loose with such invidious assertions as: "Ford's biggest problem is that I just don't think he is bright enough to be a good President." The rich and the powerful were also favored targets, it passing unremarked that "the rich" included anyone making roughly half Mondale's salary.

Public Nuisances

Yet all this must be understood not according to some strict and hopelessly antiquated moral code but according to modern political standards of discourse.

One of the most treasured insights of the modern pol is: ideas have no consequences, nor do words. The successful pol chooses words not for their denotation but for their connotation. In modern political discourse words often have only flavor and aroma—no calories and no consequences. Some words are poison, and the pol, if he is serious about entrancing the voters and staying in office, avoids these words. Instead he resorts to the good words, and the Great Solemnizer knows them all. He richly flavors his elocutions with such words as "equality," "justice," "decency," "fairness," and "compassion." He strings together luscious confections like "the politics of human need," "problem-solver," "fair share," and "problem-oriented, pragmatic liberal," and he watches his audiences of schoolmarms, librarians, bureaucrats, and other social barnacles roll in delight. Release these words but for an instant, and the room is full of heavenly fragrances. Soon everyone within hearing range is rendered ineffably lovey-dovey, and around the speaker can be heard the fluttering of angels' wings.

Mr. Mondale's audiences hear the angelic sough often, for not only does he have excellent taste in words but he maintains an ample stock of oratorical flourishes, masterpieces of political speciousness. One of his most favored is to demand increased expenditures for this or that high-minded swindle, while insisting that these expenditures will actually amount to a stupendous savings for the sorely pressed taxpayer. Exhortations for ever more bureaucracy are often supported by the argument that such expansion will mean greater governmental efficiency, less political chicanery, more responsiveness, and greater personal liberty. Though Mondale is one of the most

earnest advocates of collectivism, during election years he gets
to be somewhat of a bore about the virtues of free enterprise
and less governmental penetration of the private sector. Mondale may be the Treasury's most feared spendthrift, but when
the rhetorical fevers are on him he is a genuine fussbudget
about balanced budgets and tax relief. All this evasion and
contradiction works marvels in Minnesota where as many as
50 percent of the voters perceive him as a conservative, a perception that has never been disputed by the "problem-
oriented, pragmatic liberal."

Not surprisingly, he used these oratorical gifts to their fullest
when he joined Mr. Carter on the National Salvation ticket in
1976. An exchange with a *Newsweek* interviewer in July of
that great year is illuminating. Asked where he, a renowned
busing advocate, sent his children to school, he proclaimed
most proudly: "I'm one of the few senators whose children
have gone to public schools." Having released that anesthe-
tizing puff, he added a minor qualification: the Mondales no
longer attend public schools. No, he freed them from public
schools earlier—for he and Joan had judged that "those
schools were just not delivering what we thought was a minimum decent education for our children. The issue was the
quality of education." This is the kind of elevated judgment
permissible only to men whose largeness of spirit has already
been proven by a life predicated on decency and integrity.
When others make such judgments, suspicions are aroused.
Later, when asked if there was "an element of hypocrisy in ad-
vocating busing while at the same time putting your own children in private schools," it took a tub of vaseline but the Great
Solemnizer slipped through. "First of all I am not an advocate
of busing," said the man who from September 17 to September 25, 1975, voted seventeen times with the Senate's pro-
busing forces. "What I advocate is the elimination of discrimi-

179

nation when the courts find it." A statesmanlike testimonial, and a vivid example of modern political discourse.

On January 4, 1973, the Great Solemnizer introduced into the United States Senate an entire bill written in this deceptive argot. Called "The Full Opportunity and National Goals and Priorities Act," it adumbrated the most colossal statist undertaking ever introduced in the Senate. It also splendidly displayed the pol's contempt for intelligence and for the consequences of ideas. It represented the essence of the Mondale mentality.

Title I would establish a Council of Social Advisors and a national "social report," while adopting "full opportunity as a national goal." Title II would create a new congressional staff office of goals and priorities analysis, a prodigious instrument that would "equip Congress with the kind of manpower, data, and technology" to decide national social needs and clamp them down on us. The idea is as old as scientology. It grows from the social indicators movement associated with people like Alice Rivlin, Mancur Olson, Jr., and the late Raymond Bauer. It is a movement that in the past had many advocates amongst those of a technocratic inclination. Accordingly, social scientists—Mondale's Council of Social Advisors—are supposed to measure social health more or less in the way that economists (the President's Council of Economic Advisors) measure national income.

There are only three major problems here: no theory exists for such a social accounting; there is no consensus on what quantities one would measure in making such a social accounting; and, assuming one could take a social accounting, its helpfulness would be problematic. For instance, in attempting to measure a society's physical health what do we include? Do we measure longevity, life expectancy at birth, death rates by causes, hospital admissions, infant mortality rates, days of disability? With regard to disability, do we measure short-term or long-term disability? What of partial disability? What of psychological disability? What is psychological disability? Are there not other conditions we might measure with respect to health, and will these conditions remain static?

The believer in the national indicators hokum claims that one can make an index of all these things, giving each its proper weight in the general measurement. But, of course, this weighing would be purely arbitrary, so what would the index mean? Everything would be weighted according to caprice. There is no reasonable basis for deciding the weight of infant mortality against, say, days of disability on the part of adults. Conceptually, it is preposterous to think one can come up with a number that represents in a significant or interesting way such a complicated and disparate set of conditions. Nevertheless, the notion of settling on one number to show "American Health" is powerfully alluring to social tinkerers. It would serve as a national thermometer for American health, and the Council of Social Advisors could magisterially announce that health is up a point or down a point, and that something vast and urgent must be done; but what?

Assuming this social measurement were possible, one would have to prove its relevance to the electorate, and then a legislative remedy would have to be fashioned, passed, and enforced. What will we do if some citizens refuse to comply? Is it unreasonable to expect that large numbers of Americans would ignore a nutritional law limiting personal sugar consumption or barring alcohol? Today there exists broad agreement on the hazard of cigarettes. Yet Congress has not banned them. In fact it has subsidized tobacco growers. Admittedly, the day might come sometime off in the authoritarian dawn when our government outlaws tobacco; but are we, a society that is decriminalizing marijuana, really going to make cigarette smoking illegal? Assuming a nation's physical health could be measured, imagine the enormous amount of legislation, regulation, and police activity demanded to enforce a broad national health standard. And health is only one social condition Mondale would measure. His Council of Social Advisors would simultaneously be composing social index numbers for crime, child rearing, mobility, aging, work satisfaction, juvenescing, cheerfulness, the quality of life amongst the giant redwoods, and so on into eternity.

The Full Opportunity and National Goals and Priorities Act would leave us with a bureaucracy empowered to keep society in an incessant pother and to snoop into every area of a citizen's life. Every "social report" published by the Council of Social Advisors would trumpet some new and overwhelming crisis. At a minimum, Mondale would have established a bureaucracy to thump for his brand of statist policies whether he and his kind were in or out of office. In sheer technocratic hubris this abominable bill is the domestic equivalent of our magnificently managed Vietnam war, a war Mondale supported until 1969.

All this weighs heavily against him, yet when all is said and undone I really have to salute him. The kind of government he has hollered for during all these years would present us with an infinitely more entertaining spectacle than anything President Carter will ever heave up. It could even outdo the political science of Field Marshal Idi Amin Dada, or His Excellency Emperor Bokassa I of the progressive Central African Empire.

Mondale is the child of that brand of liberalism that in its moral imperialism disrupts every human relationship and unhinges every human value. It envisions a dizzy polity in which no one would have any solid expectation regarding such mundane matters as his education, his home, his work, his marriage. At any moment, Mondalian liberalism could send large sections of the population off in some high-minded pursuit of justice or improved health or better social adjustment. Once, Mondale was a burning anti-Communist; today he is an anti-anti-Communist. Once, he opposed racial prejudice; today he favors the government-sanctioned racial prejudice of quotas. Yesterday he thought education should bring all Americans up to a certain level of sophistication; today he feels education should descend to the yahoo's level and not be elitist.

Forever demanding more power in the federal government, he apparently fails to notice that thanks to him and his kind we now have a government with more brute power than ever before. Yet it is a hopeless flummox: a ganglion of power that in some instances overwhelms, yet in other instances is without efficacy or purpose or perception or the ability to discriminate. The Age of Mondale would be a superb show of dizziness and bathos. The bombast and mindlessness would be a marvel. How well I remember May 7, 1971, when the Great Solemnizer rose to the podium to declare: "the sickening truth is that this country is rapidly coming to resemble South Africa. . . . the native reserves and Bantustans are the inner city, and our apartheid is all the more disgusting for being insidious and unproclaimed." Mondale was speaking to the Law Institute of the NAACP Legal Defense and Educational Fund. He knew what they wanted to hear. "To begin with," he said, "the Federal Government played a major role in building ghettos and creating this isolation. . . . The Federal Government's involvement in residential segregation was not a matter of inadvertence or neglect. It was conscious, stated policy." And just which senators were behind this "conscious, stated policy" to have the federal government build these vast housing projects

within the inner city (urban renewal I believe it was called)?
Which senators were behind so many other federal policies
that by the mid- and late 1970s had aroused the scorn of Mondale and his allies? Good questions these, and so let us leave
the bright young man from metropolitan Elmore, hollering at
the top of his lungs, looking ever forward, and never looking
back. His is the voice of progress.

22

Andrew Young:
The Black Man's Burden

THOUGH our nation abounds with gifted men there is only one whom President Carter extolled as a "great man." This lonely Americano was described by the *New York Times* as cool, intelligent, and articulate; whereupon he duly sired such learned sonorities as: "I believe in neocolonialism when it's moving in the right direction," "Trying to be independent of the rest of the world is to commit suicide," and "Chaos occurs when human rights are not respected"—a useful apothegm if one will but banish from mind Eastern Europe, the Soviet Union, and China, the quietest quarter of the earth's surface. Not only is he an American Churchill, but he is a reformer with brains: "So even if we have a Foreign Service that's extremely well trained academically, there hasn't been much sensitivity training." There you are, sensitivity training for the State Department! What could more effectively ingratiate our diplomatic corps to the foreign ministries of the world than the squirrelly look of Esalen-trained me-freaks?

Public Nuisances

Whose mellow wisdom is this? The glow is unmistakable: in mind a precocious seven-year-old, in emotions a feature writer for *Ms.* magazine, in beliefs a full professor at Antioch College who has never doubted anything ever published in the *Nation*—you have just sampled the sententious genius of Mr. Andrew Jackson Young, B.S., B.D., our eloquent and enlightened UN Ambassador. He is America's greatest moment in diplomacy, greater even than Woodrow of the Fourteen Points. He is a moral shout heard through an immoral night. He is New Thought unflawed by the dead hand of custom. He is a nincompoop, and that ritualistic liberals praise him for just those qualities he so picturesquely lacks should give all black men premonitions regarding their retirement plans. This phenomenon of praising a black man for incapacities that would not be tolerated in a white man makes me apprehensive about the future of racial harmony in the Great Republic; and remember: my color has yet to be established by Health, Education and Welfare. If I am black, which I may indeed be, it reassures me not at all that liberals treat me as an object worthy of their formulaic patronizing but never worthy of the respect implicit in courteous criticism. The liberals' treatment of Andy and his treatment of his job gravely threaten the prospect of a wholesome community ever emerging from our racial differences. Consider Andy, the man, and his words. His eminence tells us much about the dizzy state of racial relations today.

While in his cocoon our present UN Ambassador studied the Christian occult at the famed Hartford Theological Seminary. There was laid the theological foundation that would years later support his magisterial declaration on morality: "Morality for me is thinking clearly through the alternatives, and making a decision that is best for the largest number of people." There too he studied the Great Books and got a

2,000-volt charge of social consciousness. How the jolt is administered remains concealed amongst the arcana of the liberal theologians. But every socially sensitive cleric must undergo it if he is to be fortified against the murderous conventionalities of middle-class life and allowed to realize his full potential as a pest. For Andrew Young these were the bookish years, and he emerged from them with an unshakable grasp of what appears to be liberal Christianity's key tenet, namely: Christ was a half-wit.

Soon he was awarded a collar from the United Church of Christ, Inc., and thither he advanced into a life of Christian endeavor; he took a position at the headquarters of the National Council of Churches. There he administered to the athletic programs and the media programs and stood ready to assist in every other area of spiritual exigency. He moved into civil rights, then politics. He entered Congress in 1972 and four years later was in the command post during that populist explosion that brought the Wonderboy to the White House. For Andy these were times of worldly whirl, yet how *au courant* he remained with modern theological developments can be seen in his rigorously thought-out ukase for the heathens at *Playboy:* "My faith is that all men can be saved, but I didn't want Hitler to be saved, and I don't want Idi Amin to be saved." Who has offered a more vivid encapsulation of the modern Christian love ethic?

The major intellectual influence on the Rev. Young's life has been Mr. Mohandas K. Gandhi, the Indian luminary whose spinning wheels and communal principles have brought such remarkable progress, vigor, and personal liberty to the vast subcontinent. The Mahatma's canon has long been revered by activist clerics of the Rev. Young's species, but the Rev. Young's infatuation appears to have been nearly total. In fact, he has revealed that during his Hartford period young

Public Nuisances

Andy—a future congressman!—actually contemplated a life of celibacy. Even his victualizing fell under the Mahatma's influence, and to this day he follows, albeit loosely, the dietary precepts of Adelle Davis, the Hoosier nutritionist now deceased. What other residues remain from his Gandhian immersion are subject to speculation. Formal civil disobedience remains problematic for a UN Ambassador, even one of Mr. Young's audacity, and his public statements are refreshingly vacant of those pedagogical references that made his predecessor, Mr. Daniel P. Moynihan, so hard to take. Yet Mr. Young is always at pains to remind interviewers of his debt to the Mahatma, and perhaps it is not beyond the borders of our present meditation to recall that during his public life Mr. Gandhi was something more than your average "great soul." He prescribed and administered enemas. In point of fact, rarely did there pass a day when the Mahatma failed to query his comely female attendants as to the comparative merits of their morning bowel movements. Mr. Gandhi, like Mr. Young, was not an assiduous reader, but when he hit upon a tome that impressed him he would quote from it fulsomely. For years his favorite was *Constipation and Our Civilization*, a book whose value time has somehow obscured, but one often pressed upon incredulous visitors to the Mahatma's Sevegram hermitage. I would like to have been in the library of the Hartford Theological Seminary when a pensive Mr. Young came upon *this* biographical information. Constipation has never been one of Andy's problems.

He is a popinjay of nigh unto constant fluency, and when he speaks it is as though the contents of Webster's Third have gone on a rampage. He is the kind of periphrastic maniac that even an Eisenhower might find inscrutable. His favored medium is the interview. There he is asked all manner of ques-

tion and with the pluck worthy of a Rotary boomer from Du-
buque he has at them. Rarely does he speak in sentences or
even phrases; rather he emits enormous gobs of verbiage, all
affixed precariously to those puny slivers of intellection that at
asylums like the Hartford Theological Seminary pass for ideas.
Absolutely no question is beyond his ken. He assaults them all
by summoning up some clever platitude only to lose it in a
morass of utterly meaningless elaboration or to have it tram-
pled by his own brutal contradiction. Memorable was the time
he explained his charge that Presidents Nixon and Ford were
racists: "They were racists not in the aggressive sense but in

189

that they had no understanding of the problems of colored peoples anywhere. . . . We've got to start talking about racism without putting moral categories on it so we can understand it."

Because he is adept in moral sophistry he is given to depicting in breath-catchingly portentous tones such sheer and unredeemable imbecilities as the following, which is best read with timpani rumbling just offstage: "The problems blacks face today are the problems whites will face in a couple of years. Public education, for instance. Black problems there only symbolize the fact that the whole system never has made the adjustment to a modern, urban America." In that statement Andy has a perfect score: everything about it is wrong.

Andy is apparently haunted by a proclivity for introducing that precise line of argument most likely to blast apart his own case. Even President Carter must have laughed aloud when, during the famed *Playboy* interview, Andy accused one of his favorite targets, Mr. Henry Kissinger, of flagrant ignorance regarding racism. Gently, the interviewer reminded Andy that as a Jew who had grown up in Hitler's Germany the former secretary of state "surely knows something about racism." Whereupon Andy promptly ambushed himself. Having earlier established that his experiences at the hands of Southern racists made him an expert on racism, he now declared that victims of racism are so traumatized by it that it deludes them. An even more hilarious instance of his gift for polemical autointoxication occurred when he defended the Cuban presence in Angola to a CBS interviewer: "Q. If it was wrong for the United States to be in Vietnam, why isn't it wrong for the Cubans to be in Angola? A. The Cubans were in Angola at the invitation of . . . the MPLA and . . . Q. We were in Vietnam at the invitation of a series of governments—South Vietnamese. A. You got me there. . . ." On national television,

"You got me there"! Not even Warren Gamaliel Harding suffered through such a moment.

What is more, Andy has no sense that words have meanings defined by authorities other than himself. In fact, my guess is that he uses hundreds, perhaps thousands, of words whose meanings he has only the vaguest hold on. Certainly this is suggested by the following absurd harvest culled from his public bloviations: "I demoralize racism and call it ethnocentrism"; "I really believe in meeting with anybody and everybody. But the only person I'd be reticent about meeting with is Idi Amin"; "I just can't operate on a *quid pro quo* basis. If I can't establish a line of trust, I'd rather not be bothered." The stupendously juvenile hauteur wafting from this last botch is characteristic, for Andy is the victim of a grandiose and stultifying arrogance.

The arrogance is understandable enough. During all those years of fighting the South's Jim Crow laws Andy was in a morally unassailable position. Time and again he was up against barbarians like Mr. Eugene ("Bull") Connor. Andy was a young man then, yet almost always he was dealing with his moral inferiors. Still, such experiences do not necessarily deepen one's character, and by the time Andy entered national politics in the 1970s the moral questions had become more complicated. Moreover, with the collapse of Jim Crow, the black man's problems became more subtle, and perhaps more intractable. Their ill-conceived premises aside, Andy's raucous and dizzy homilies on racism are simply irrelevant to the civil-rights movement today. The black man does not need the moralistic prattle and psychological pish-posh so popular with Andy and his chichi liberal friends. Today blacks need job-training, an expanding economy, and as few regulations barring individual industry as possible. The inner city must be able to offer today's immigrants the same opportunities open to immigrants of the past. Crime must be controlled and order restored. For today's civil-rights movement, Andy is as obsolete as Marcus Garvey and Father Divine.

Early in 1977, he had hardly delivered his first lecture against "knee-jerk anticommunism" or discovered his first racist under the bed, when ritualistic liberals began elbowing each other aside and issuing laudations to his eloquence and intelligence. "Young is a cool and pragmatic politician with a far-flung network of contacts and a quarterback's sense of timing," intoned Joseph Lelyveld in the *New York Times Magazine*; and Mr. Lelyveld has a conspicuously stunted capacity for irony. The chorus of nonsense that swelled up every time Andy flummoxed the works remains a garish manifestation of the ritualistic liberals' uneasy acceptance of blacks, and an arresting illustration of their high moral commitment to a politics of sheer symbolism and empty gestures.

Drugs, vice, and general social disintegration continue to destroy the very conception of neighborhood in our inner cities. An entire generation of young blacks is in danger of passing into adulthood without ever having acquired the tools necessary for constructive participation in modern society. A vast amount of scholarship suggests that new approaches to urban social problems are necessary, the older solutions having quite possibly worsened the urban condition. Yet the ritualistic liberals whoop it up every time Andy abandons himself to an impulse increasingly pronounced amongst American public figures, to wit: the impulse to ham it up and make an ass of oneself. By agglutinating the rhetoric of the 1960s civil-rights movement with the personal liberationist rhetoric and the rhetoric of almost every other trendy leftish enthusiasm known to Beverly Hills, Andy has led much of the civil-rights movement away from the real needs of the minority poor and toward the fanciful needs of the salon revolutionaries and the self-realization bores.

During his first six months in office Andy sounded as though he were Special Ambassador to the UN from *Cosmopolitan* magazine. He has never improved. In his initial outbursts he reiterated the discredited revisionist canards about American responsibility for the Cold War. He lectured Americans for being "paranoid" about Communism in Africa. And he absolved the hooligans who in a famous rampage looted lower-middle-class shops in New York, asseverating that ". . . if you turn the lights out folks will steal. They'll do that in Switzerland, too, especially if they're hungry." Then Andy played "Variations on a Theme of Racism" to the amusement and bewilderment of the world. The Swedes were "terrible racists," the British quite possibly had "invented racism," the Russians were "the worst racists in the world," and Queens was as hellish as Sweden. "No one who knows him, however, would question his diplomatic skills," the judicious Mr. Lelyveld had said. God knows what Mr. Lelyveld's judgment was a year later when Andy asserted that the tragic plight of Soviet dissidents was comparable to the condition of protestors in the United States and then uttered this prodigy: "After all, in our prisons as well there are hundreds, perhaps even thousands of people whom I would call political prisoners. I myself was sentenced ten years ago in Atlanta for having organized a protest movement." Andy had been arrested for disrupting emergency garbage collection in Atlanta; he was jailed for less than twenty-four hours.

Within six months of his UN appointment every washroom attendant in New York knew that Andy was a lightweight; but if they were to read the encomiums pouring in from the liberal brethren, large numbers of them would be growing sideburns, reading French menus, and otherwise preparing for careers in high public office. "America's newest, freshest celebrity," trumpeted *New Times*. "Hope-inspiring . . . cool, articulate, reliable," crooned the *Saturday Review*. All over the country ritualistic liberals were dreaming up esoteric arguments gainsaying the obvious, namely, that Andy was a mindless popinjay. But the most remarkable statement came from a Mr. Julius Lester, who asserted: "The continuing calls for the resignation of United Nations Ambassador Andrew Young are a sad but real reminder that a particularly pernicious kind of racism is alive and well. This is the racist mechanism which unconsciously expects and demands that any black in a position previously or usually occupied by a white conduct him or herself as whites wish, i.e., act, think, and be like a white person." Is Mr. Lester saying that all blacks are as vain and foolish as Andy, or is he saying that blacks and whites have such disparate cultural values that no understanding or intelligent communication can exist between them? Neither position is satisfactory.

Thirteen years after the 1964 Civil Rights Act, Andy and his supporters managed to trivialize the discussion of race so completely that every bigot in the country was suddenly indebted to them. Of course, Americans have misused the word "racism" for over a decade, often employing it where the term "racial prejudice" was apposite. But Andy drained it of almost all its remaining poison: "I certainly didn't mean anything derogatory," he declared after calling presidents Nixon and Ford racists. Republicans were not assuaged, and as they howled for his job he scrambled for forgiveness, explaining that racism, the terrible judgment he had been visiting on so many, was merely an "insensitivity to cultural differences." Presumably the NAACP and the Anti-Defamation League can now turn their efforts to producing travelogues. Belsen and Auschwitz might never have been built had Hitler been a member of The Club Mediterranée or a reader of *Gourmet* magazine.

Today the prospects for racial harmony are not sunny. It is customary and socially approved to discuss matters of race in terms that are almost exclusively subjective, sentimental, and excessive. Liberals have little that is sensible to say about race, conservatives say nothing about race, and a pathetico like Andy is held up as wise and imperative. It is hard to imagine how such conditions can do anything other than encourage racial prejudice. Even more worrisome is the acceptance of the idea that blacks be left just 10 or 11 percent of the Republic's professional positions. To adopt this quota system is to place blacks in an enduringly antagonistic stance toward the white majority and quite probably to condemn many of them to mediocrity. It is to certify once and probably for all those two societies, "one black, one white—separate and unequal," that the Kerner Commission spied in 1968. For how will such a system ever be ended, when, and by whom? With it established that government is to decide the extent of a group's social participation, blacks will be in a perilous situation. They are the beneficiaries of moral fervor today; they could easily be its victims tomorrow. Ours is a turbulent society and the moral fervor of liberals is famous for its inconstancy.

The spectacle of Andy Young has been produced by liberal racism and the aforementioned impulse of American eminentoes to ham it up in the trashiest manner imaginable. Every civilized spectator has enjoyed this show, but not without a twinge of apprehension. Andy was once one of the most influential blacks in the Republic. Today he is the black man's burden.

23

Joseph Califano:
An Encomium

THAT NOT ONE notable in all of Washington rejoiced at the incongruity of raising up a hustler to preside over the largest governmental department of do-goodery in Christendom I take to be exquisite evidence attesting to one of my most dearly held convictions, to wit: we live under a near-tyranny of humorless minds. Think of it. On December 23, 1976, just plain ole Jimmy tapped Mr. Joseph A. Califano, Jr., to head the Department of Health, Education and Welfare, yet no one in Washington was startled. In the service of Jimmy, the Washington outsider, Califano—a Washington insider of unsmiteable energy and acquisitiveness—departs Georgetown to take over the nation's loaves and fishes operation; yet there is no serenade of guffaws, no general outburst of facetiae. One might have expected ho-ho-ho's all the days of Joe's tenure, but the news commentators reported his appointment with strenuous sobriety, and then became his faithful PR agents. I believe that America is afflicted by humorless minds whose influence towers out of all proportion to their number. I believe that these rascals are not only blind to preposterosity but intent on intimidating into gloom all those with a proclivity for cheer. And I believe that the day will come when it will be either us or them.

Witness Joe's arrival at HEW: professional poverty experts by the hundreds peer down from their windows as up the drive he comes, encased in his limousine, followed by a gorgeous retinue. There can be seen his $78,225-per-year bodyguard, there his $12,763-per-year cook, there a former vice-president of Harvard University. Others follow. How can one view such a spectacle and not break up?

I am sure that Joe saw the humor in it, and that is why he fetches my approbation. He is absolutely shameless. He has down pat all the rhetoric of the constituency-of-conscience crowd, and he still maintains his table at Sans Souci. He weeps with them, he roars on their behalf, he navigates every blind turn in their zigzagging public philosophy—he prospers. I have never seen a picture of him that there was not a twinkle in his brown eyes. His ample cheeks fairly glow with bonhomie. Is he arrogant? To be sure. And secretive? Naturally. Does he work eighteen-hour days, bullying his employees and incessantly expanding his influence? *Mais bien sûr.* All this is true, but it does not gainsay my claim that Joe is, deep within, a clever and jolly soul. He sees greater Washington for the farce that it is, and he enjoys the act. He knows that the bureaucrats over which he rules are born mules to be goaded and manipulated. He senses the vacuity of the average pol, he turns it to his own account, and he does it with gusto. My guess is that he takes especial pleasure in exploiting Washington's lobbyists of uplift. They are the most humorless hinds of all, and nothing could be more entertaining and profitable than using their own canards to enslave them.

Public Nuisances

In the late 1950s Joe spent a couple of sad years practicing law on Wall Street. That was quite enough for him. His wife, the former Gertrude Zawacki, apprised him of the amusing grandeur of the New Frontier, whereupon he shook his barristerial chains and sought out the Kennedy promise. That is to say, he sought out the good life via humbug and the taxing power. Joe has never left Washington. During the Kennedy years when names like Sorensen and Salinger graced the top of the marquee, Joe selflessly put himself to the task of learning the angles. Practically all the celebrated New Frontiersmen came a cropper, but Joe matured. He kept his nose to the *Zeitgeist*. Today he must be considered Kennedyism's most accomplished and enduring practitioner, always feverishly throwing himself into noble causes, always flattering the *popolo minuto* with heroic guff, and never missing an opportunity to snatch a bit more of their freedom and their loot. Contradictions between his past promises and present posturings never slow him down, and no one seems to mind. Was he not one of those LBJ aides responsible for domestic intelligence operations against civil-rights activists, black militants, and antiwar protestors? The April 17, 1971, *New York Times* confirms it. Did he not yell and wail with affecting fury over Nixon's domestic intelligence intrigues? He did it on the op-ed page of the very *Times*—there and anywhere else he could get a foot in the door.

His has been a life of inconsistencies brazenly and cheerfully ignored. In 1976 our populist president summoned him to redistribute the wealth, to regulate the Rockefeller impulse that throbs in us all, and to clamp down hard on those robber barons then in league with the devious American Medical Association. During that year Joe had earned $561,215, nearly $500,000 of it from one pharmaceutical company. "We need desperately in this country to redistribute more wealth," Joe

notified the *Christian Science Monitor,* and he knows whereof
he remonstrates. In his last year of private practice this interesting man earned more than General Motors chairman
Thomas Murphy, the fifteenth highest-paid business executive
in America. In the eighteen years from 1960 to 1978 Joe spent
scarcely seven practicing law, and then he had but four
clients. Nonetheless he became a millionaire. Still, our president asked him to patrol the provinces of excess profits, exploi-
tative health care, and man's inhumanity to man. These matters he now ponders from his box at Washington Redskins
football games with Mr. Art Buchwald, Herblock, and other
members of the Washington intelligentsia. This is *hilaritas!*

One of Joe's favorite areas for reform is health care, and for
years he has bedeviled the health-care tycoons. In 1976 he
handed one pharmaceutical company the largest bill for services rendered that company had ever received. Six months
later he walloped the health-care crowd once again, declaring
to an uneasy assemblage of the American Medical Association:
"There is virtually no competition among doctors or among
hospitals. . . . There is precious little competition among
pharmaceutical companies or among laboratories [whose] research has become big business, with patent monopoly pots of
gold at the end of the research rainbow"—pots of gold demanding the professional services of sharp Washington lawyers, let us hasten to add. The docs were discomfited, but they
were not surprised. A month earlier Joe had struck at the hospital moguls, urging that it become *malum prohibitum* for
hospitals to raise rates by more than 9 percent annually. If his
suggestion were made law would the consequent loss in hospital services affect Joe? HEW provides. In fact its chief has
access to a whole stable of specialists on twenty-four-hour call
lest the chief stagger. In 1977 an HEW physician en route to
his summer vacation was actually ordered back to Washington

to attend to his ailing boss. Joe had been felled by the tragedy of "tennis wrist." Hospital costs may indeed be barred from rising more than 9 percent annually, but one can be sure that no loss of service will be suffered at Bethesda Naval Hospital or at any other hospital reserved for our government's elite. Our pols and top bureaucrats must be kept in the pink and with minimum delay. Cost can be no object lest they be distracted from improving our condition.

Joe has had to hustle all his days, yet he has shown that the thing can be carried off with *joie de vivre* and with brass. No wizened slave to the Protestant ethic is he. Joe is living proof that one of Washington's legendary "workaholics" can be cheerful. In fact he is famous for joshing it up with reporters, pols, and anyone else who might someday be useful and who is not directly subordinate to him.

The grandchild of an immigrant fruitmonger, Joe bounced about the hard surfaces of Brooklyn, graduated from Holy Cross, and entered Harvard Law School, from which he emerged *magna cum laude* after honing his legalese at the *Harvard Law Review.*

In the Kennedy administration he served as a button-down factotum, first for a Mr. Cy Vance and then for Mr. Robert S. McNamara, the theorist. Joe was quick to grasp the change Kennedy was bringing about. Soon Washington would be transformed from a drowsy Southern city of boozy pols into a world capital, the seat of the most immense government on the planet. In the years to come behemoth bureaucracies would be shelved in gigantic and hideous buildings—every one looking like a fortress designed by Le Corbusier. Politics was already becoming America's safest route to riches and fun; and political influence for the nonelected, and probably nonelectable, could be secured by showering one's boss with memos, ramrodding whatever idiotic policy is presumed to as-

suage the crisis of the moment, and solemnly intoning whatever socially approved bromides suddenly become fashionable
amongst the powerful.

These were important components of the Kennedy style.
Henry Fairlie has pointed out that the Kennedys "could not sit
still"; and Joe found a political philosóphy based on harum-
scarum much to his liking. Of course his language is not
always as grandiloquent as that of JFK, but it has plenty of
noble exhortations, spiced with nonce values like compassion
and progress. Moreover, let us remember that even the elegant
JFK was not above blurting out such bilge as "The American
cow is the 'foster mother' of the human race, and a great asset
to the nation"—the historic day was February 27, 1960, and
the site, Bloomer, Wisconsin 54724.

Joe became renowned for tireless activity and thousands
(perhaps hundreds of thousands) of memos. I have it on good
authority that the gentle Cy Vance would huddle behind his
chair whenever a caravan arrived from Joe's office. McNamara
was more agreeable to bumbledom and Johnson seems to have
positively envied it—though on this the historians are in dispute. Some say the truckloads of memos sent up for LBJ's nocturnal reading made him groan. Others insist that Johnson admired the prolific young memoist, fending off any criticism of
him with statements like: "Don't you criticize Califano.
There's never been a man around me who wrote so many
memos."

This anecdote is useful, revealing as it does the Washington
exaltés' high esteem for that neurotic frenzy that they take to
be an acceptable simulacrum for work, and, alas, suggesting
Joe's mixed reviews. Sad to say, not everyone appreciated the
rising hustler. Some went so far as to allege that he unscrupu-
lously claimed authorship of memos actually written by subor-
dinates. This is a charge that ought to be laid to rest once and

for all. Fortunately, its merits are not too difficult to establish. Joe's prose style is outstanding, even for a Washington operator. The distinguishing mark that gives it away every time is that some variation of the word "enhance" appears on every third page. At any rate, I can well imagine the surreptitious amusement Joe derived from advancing himself through governmental ranks by creating ever more onerous labor for his bosses. There is before my mind's eye a vivid image of him merrily trundling around the halls of government, gathering bushel baskets of incomprehensible facts and dubious analyses, pasting them down and tying them together with portentous and hopelessly wrongheaded conclusions, then ordering some twitching ninety-pound secretary to lug them off to his already sorely pressed boss. It is the kind of joke Joe enjoys best: putting to his own purposes the foolishness of the hour.

This has always been his strong suit: give the clowns what dazzles them. Joe is neither a conservative nor a liberal; he is a public servant who chooses his publics wisely. During his great years he has presciently sensed the changing moods and has generally latched on to those gifted men who were about to change these moods. No about-face has been beyond his God-given talents. Joe keeps his face to the horizon. His past does not trouble him. Nowadays in America this is an essential quality for greatness.

At first his policy responsibilities were tedious matters like supervising the Army Corps of Engineers' Civil Works Program and monitoring the water-pollution-control regulations. Yet even in these dreary hours he must have enjoyed himself. There is that absurd earnestness with which government's career bureaucrats pursue hopeless and often contradictory policies. Doubtless he entertained himself with mischievous subterfuges just to make their work grimmer and more idiotic. Perhaps he set them to doing those pointless studies of mass transit; after all, he had a hand in the establishment of the Department of Transportation. Then, too, I can see him personally rewriting regulatory codes, making them even more incomprehensible to bureaucrats and the regulated alike. And then, of course, he would holler at the oafs. Of that I am certain. His penchant for diatribes is one of his most ingratiating traits.

Under Johnson, Joe rose to become one of the most powerful White House aides in history. Newspapers were given to calling him "deputy president of the Great Society," though his formal appellation was "special assistant for domestic affairs." By 1967 he was probably Johnson's top aide—Walter Jenkins, Bobby Baker, and Bill Moyers having already made their contributions to our history—and no one doubts that he was chief architect of many Great Society programs. Not only did he have a hand in water-pollution control, but by 1967 he was deeply involved in more exciting mischief like the so-called consumer legislation, automobile safety, the Office of Economic Opportunity, and possibly the most notable botch of all, Model Cities.

On leaving office he joined up with the hottest political law firm in Washington, Arnold and Porter, and spent the next couple of years leading business clients across the tricky terrain of government regulations, many of which he knew from the inside out, so to speak. In 1971 he continued this service when he started his own law firm with Edward Bennett Williams, controller of the Washington Redskins. Yet as always Joe could not sit still. Between clients he played politics in the gardens of the Democrats and wrote two books: a slim and banal volume titled *The Student Revolution: A Global Confrontation* (1970), and a thick and banal volume titled *A Presidential Nation* (1975). In the first he batters the "establishment" for its insensitivity to student aspirations in the 1960s; in the second he frets over the awesome power that Richard Nixon somehow managed to gather about the presidency. The most striking feature of both books is that they treat issues which at the time of publication horrified ritualistic liberals. What is more, Joe discusses these crises in terms decidedly pleasing to the ritualistic liberals without ever revealing his role in bringing the crises to life.

His achievement here cannot be overstated. Nor should we miss the importance of these books in saving a dangerously imperiled career and in illuminating the workings of Joe's clever mind. They were written in dark times when a new spirit of impious brainlessness threatened to take over the Democratic Party and to finish off everyone ever associated with that party's *ancien régime*. Joe had not only lived it up in Versailles, he had helped to build the place. Yet by masterfully playing to every inflection of the current wisdom he managed to put himself on good terms with the mob. Less than a year after publication of the second book he was back in power.

All this was accomplished with his customary blatancy. In the first book Joe frankly admits that he has just hit up the Ford Foundation for an around-the-world trip and that the drivel he has ladled out is the result of "essentially impressionistic" stops in places like Rome, Paris, and London. It is a cheeky admission and not without its clever political purpose, revealing as it does Joe's good repute with that august fount of social change. Knowing what we know about Joe's style of life, I can think of nothing more fattening than to have accompanied him on these researches. Imagine how much greater a contribution to knowledge this book would have made if it had been written on "Great Restaurants: A Global Phenomenon." Alas, such a volume will have to await a shift in the left-liberal canon of concerns. Such shifts are not unthinkable—some suffering situation could turn up at the Tour d'Argent, and if it does, doubtless Joe will be there to inform us.

Joe's tenure at HEW might be slightly less exciting than his career under LBJ. Gigantic social programs are still talked about, but there is a troubling reluctance in the Congress to pass them. Moreover, today's urgent questions of justice call for more subtle policies like ridding American high schools of such vestiges of bigotry as father-son dinners. These activities can be amusing, especially in the case of affirmative action where one can totally disrupt the lives of millions of stuffy middle-class drones and at times personally thrust an utter incompetent upon his superiors. After all who knows better than Joe what is best for the flotsam and jetsam? Today he must positively exult in decrying health hazards such as alcoholic beverages, chocolate cream pies, and tobacco—the latter, incidentally, being an industry in which, so the newspapers say, he has considerable amounts of stock.

Whether such comparatively low-key mischief amuses Joe is not recorded. Doubtless he would truly like to get on with the spending of more billions and with serving as the architect of an even greater Great Society, but for now this is not to be. Joe's 1960s handiwork is already running the country into bankruptcy and word of its worthlessness is spreading.

No less reliable a source than the Brookings Institution reviewed Joe's work back in the spring of 1972 and proclaimed the Great Society full of mold. Traditional big government programs of the New Deal type were plausible, for the knowledge needed to transfer money to the needy or to build dams has been around for a long time. Great Society endeavors, however, like programs for improving health care, preschool education, and job training, were more difficult. They often involved unacceptable amounts of coercion and knowledge that did not exist. For instance, no one really knows how to raise reading achievement scores in poverty schools. These kinds of problems coupled with high costs make it unlikely that Joe will get another fling at his favorite kind of activity.

Yet there is still plenty to do. From 1963 to 1973, spending for Great Society programs soared from $1.7 billion to $35.7 billion, and since then it has more than doubled. Today Joe has more money to spend, more people to manipulate, and more areas in which to intrude. Public service should continue to attract him. He is one of the most successful and I believe joyful men to come to Washington in the past twenty-five years. I predict he will continue to skip along his blessed path. He is one of God's darlings.

24

Ralph Nader:
Return of the Shakers

R ALPH NADER, LL.B., is neither a scientist, a philosopher, an economist, nor an epicurean. He sleeps but four
hours a night, goes for days sustained solely by an occasional
cookie or banana, and practices strict celibacy midst a catastrophe of file cabinets and yellowing newspapers in his legendary
eighty-five-dollar-a-month Washington, D.C., apartment. It
is unclear exactly what his judgment of the domestic pizza pie
might be. Mexican food also resides in a limbo of scholarly
speculation. But Wonder Bread is sinister stuff, and on Coca-
Cola Citizen Nader is eloquent and adamantine. When the
Great Emancipator from Plains, Georgia, refused publicly to
sever his connection with the Atlanta-based multinational
menace, there was considerable perturbation at Nader, Inc.
Hot dogs are *malum in se,* and God does not will that mankind
sit to the fore of the internal combustion engine, but rather
that he sit astern it and always tightly swaddled in a seat belt,
preferably of the advanced inertia variety. The efficient pro-

duction of goods and services is beyond the pale to Citizen Nader, as are sleep, reflective thought, careful research, prudent discourse, courteous manners, and tolerance. The qualities one is most likely to encounter in the upwardly mobile Naderist are bloodshot eyes, insomnia, chronic stomach disorder, a choleric disposition, anti-intellectualism, mild Jacobinism, and no sex—in brief many of the qualities once characteristic of the Shakers.

If I have perciptiently read Citizen Nader's five lovey-dovey biographers, the aforementioned qualities are his most ingratiating. What these hagiographers judge to be his unseemly qualities I blush to think. The Nader cosmos is unlike that of any American demigod save the relatively limited cosmos of some of our religious loons. The tests that we usually apply to labor leaders, businessmen, and politicians simply are not applied to Citizen Nader. There never has been anything quite like him in this vast and diverse Republic. He is a hybrid of William Jennings Bryan and John Brown. Next to him even the ghost of San Clemente appears unexceptional.

For over a decade he has fussily scampered across America, tirelessly scolding citizens for their economics, their technology, and their government. That he has no established expertise in any of these fields is obvious. His researches are almost always flyblown and often promptly refuted once the shock of his canards has worn off. That these reports constitute one of his chief product lines does not speak very well for engineering or for quality control at Nader, Inc. If any corporation in America ever turned out such a lemon as his report on the perils of the Volkswagen, it would soon be on the road to bankruptcy with Naderists yapping all the way to the grave. Even his fabled report on the pathetic Corvair failed to hold up under scrutiny. The Department of Transportation found it full of malfunctioning "facts." *Road and Track*, an automobile magazine written mainly by disinterested engineers, found the Volkswagen report selective, tendentious, and in parts arrantly erroneous. Yet the production line at Nader, Inc. continues to roll, manned often by college students and rank amateurs, a last holdout against the child labor laws. A careful reading of his prescriptions for automotive safety suggests that Citizen Nader believes automobiles are meant to be run into concrete walls. His ideal auto would incorporate the characteristics of a Mercedes Benz 450 SEL with those of a bulldozer. Who could afford such monstrosities is a mystery; how innocent pedestrians and small buildings might survive in a world populated by them is a mystery consorting with an enigma. Yet these reports are not that much different from his other reports. He even botched his "Congress Project"—an astounding matter, that, considering the dysfunctional wrecks tottering about on Capitol Hill.

So much for his famed reports, but what of his theories and insights? Insofar as I am able to make any sense of them at all, those for which he is esteemed were all hatched long ago by such various eminences as Milton Friedman, Frank Knight, Karl Marx, and C. Wright Mills. Consider his discovery that regulatory commissions fall into the hands of those they are meant to regulate. Anyone familiar with Friedman's *Capitalism and Freedom* knows this, but no serious individual would then turn around and offer Citizen Nader's solution, to wit, establishing superregulatory agencies to oversee our present regulatory agencies. Nor do intelligent students of our economy believe that it is increasingly controlled by two hundred giant corporations, a yahoo allegation that has been around for years; too much research on market concentration, for instance by economists Paul McCracken and Harold Demsetz, has demonstrated its error. Yet Citizen Nader holds to this belief with a devotion not dissimilar from that shown by those

Public Nuisances

who believe that the world is controlled by a handful of fat bankers barricaded somewhere in the Alps. Bah! And bah to his belief that the American people are enthralled by the wizards of Madison Avenue. No research has ever proven that in a relatively free market advertising can continue to coerce consumers to purchase goods that do not satisfy them. In sum, most of his insights are misperceptions, and when he actually does come up with an intelligent insight his solution is wrong.

Nonetheless Citizen Nader continues to sound off on a breathtakingly wide range of issues, a consumerist who is celebrated for not consuming, a champion of the ecosphere who sulks when his staff breaks from its seven-day work week for a visit to the beach, an activist disdainful of intellectuals and political philosophy who finds meaning and inspiration in what every sly pol recognizes as sheer bromide: "the public interest." His decade of prosperity is one of the most preposterous success stories in American history, more absurd even than the career of Henry Wallace. His seduction of the press is perhaps somewhat understandable; after all, the press has always had a weakness for the purely weird—weird stories having the surest chance of snagging readers. But his seduction of liberalism would nearly defy rational explanation were it not for the fact that liberalism through the years has been increasingly susceptible to Puritanism, self-destruction, and a petty disrelish for commerce.

That Citizen Nader wishes to scotch business is clear for all to see. Actually, his consumerism does not so much display a love of the consumer as it betrays a truly virulent hatred of the producer. Rarely does one hear him sermonize on how the lowly consumer is fleeced by taxation and inflation. Hardly ever does he defend the consumer against the costly, inefficient beadledom of big government. And even less often does he have at it with labor unions. Instead we hear ceaseless diatribes against the infamies of businessmen, as if they were not consumers themselves. Doubtless American business can stand examination, but shoddy, diffuse reports steeped in economic and political voodoo are no service to anyone other than our nation's perpetual malcontents.

Having dutifully considered the voluminous complaints Citizen Nader has lodged against American business and American government, I have come to believe that he is discomfited by something far deeper than pollution, corruption, and booby-trapped cars. Even if Coca-Cola surrenders tomorrow, the conspiracies of General Motors are shut down forever, and Lake Erie becomes a health spa, Citizen Ralph will not be able to shake himself loose from the coils of the public interest. So long as the common folk are free to choose one value over another, for instance cheapness over safety, life will be full of treachery. So long as our democratic society tolerates diversity and resists the standardization that Nader's regulatory commissions and bureaucracies demand, safety, health, and reform will be thwarted. Freedom and tolerance are at issue here. Citizen Nader's record as a civil libertarian is poor; the logic of his proposals casts doubt on the possibility it will ever improve. One of his dearest dreams is to eliminate smoking from federally regulated areas. Not content with the reasonable practice of segregating smokers on airplanes, he would have them totally eliminated. It is proudly claimed that he refuses to employ smokers and feels it his right to inquire into the smoking habits of potential employees. If this is his position on a discomfort as trivial as smoking how can one conclude he would be more tolerant of graver inconveniences? Would he tolerate Mennonites cluttering the public roads with their horse-drawn vehicles? Are people to be free to choose chiropractors over medical doctors?

Not only is Citizen Nader subversive to freedom and a

pluralistic society, he is also subversive to stable institutions. His zealotry on behalf of something as impalpable and protean as the public interest gives no hint as to what he might attack next. Originally he set out to reform the Corvair, then it was General Motors, then all corporations, then health care. Soon he wanted to deregulate air fares but to regulate other industries. Today he speaks ominously of scrapping the capitalist system, and in favor of what? No one knows. Such turbulence is intolerable to a liberal society. Free citizens must live with some reasonable expectations for the future. Are wage-earners gladly going to live in suspense over the fate of their banks, their insurance systems, their transportation investments? Will investors venture their savings in enterprises that may be banned tomorrow? Can laborers train themselves for jobs that may suddenly disappear by edict of this necromancer of the public interest?

Soon or late liberals are going to have to ask themselves what manner of ideologue this Citizen Nader is. For me the answer has been shouted aloud by his public record. In too many matters of choice and tolerance Citizen Nader has opted for coercion. On the matter of his liberalism and his devotion to progress he spoke volumes when he lamented in the *New York Times Magazine* that "We ask our people to think instead of asking them to believe. And history has always gone to those who ask people to believe"—*Also sprach* not Der Führer or Chairman Mao, but one of the most renowned reformers ever to rise up in the Great Democracy.

As dismaying as it might be to Citizen Nader, I personally prefer thinking persons to believers. The free and democratic society is an evolutionary step up from the paternalistic tyranny he favors. Advocates of democracy and liberalism have held that their society encourages intelligence, sentience, and responsibility, that is to say, a sturdier and better *Homo sapiens* than the poor waif slouching under the enlightened rule of an autocrat. There are some discomforts attendant here—individuals will have to make their own choices—but I prefer the discomforts of freedom to the securities of serfdom.

That liberals have missed the import of Citizen Nader's critique does not speak well for them. Character is a prelude to action; and what is the character of a man who sleeps four hours a night, snoops into the private lives of his employees, follows a teenager's dietary habits while lecturing the whole nation on health, and in the end laments that we Americans are given to thinking rather than believing? Delicacy prevents me from uttering the word, delicacy and anxiety about waking up to an army of libel lawyers. For that is another of Citizen Nader's ingratiating qualities. He is congenitally litigious, especially toward those who take issue with his causes and speak their minds. Citizen Nader is the latest edition of American Puritanism. I prefer the first edition.

25

The Hon. Teddy and the Camelot Buncombe

IT IS the palmy spring of a college boy's sophomore year. He is somewhat of a chucklehead, owing to the fragrances of the season and the rising beauty he spies whenever he approaches a mirror to subdue his stubble. Tonight there is an irresistible swelling within his epigastrium, and so he sits down to his desk and unbosoms himself thus:

"Euphoria reigned; we thought for a moment that the world was plastic and the future unlimited.

"Never had girls seemed so pretty, tunes so melodious, an evening so blithe and unconstrained."

Here, to be sure, is a sophomore on the make. A small ocean of beer will disappear and many wary coeds will render him absurd before the season passes. Yes? No!

The above sentimental skip comes from no college boy at all—my little joke, if you will. It is the production of Arthur M. Schlesinger, Jr., a Pulitzer Prize-winning historian full of years and unnumbered solemn experiences. Moreover, Arthur

The Hon. Teddy and the Camelot Buncombe

is not writing about adolescent *amour;* the screwball writes about politics! Years ago Arthur became a fool for Camelot, much as the Good Book enjoins us to become fools for Christ. When he was young, Arthur was considered the most intelligent, discerning, and readable historian of his generation, but he was chloroformed by Camelot, and for two decades this American Tacitus has been on twenty-four-hour call, always ready and willing to put a gossamer of grandeur on the empty deeds of three rogues whenever the call from Hyannis Port would come in.

Since the early 1960s the Camelot buncombe has served as ritualistic liberalism's *Tafelmusik*, reliably providing a reassuring backdrop for Arthur and his fellows as they mechanically patter on about an "equitable distribution of the wealth," the urgency of "radically reforming the system" (their system, I might add), injustice, cigarettes used indoors, and so on. Balanced minds dismiss the buncombe out of hand as a congeries of affecting illusions adhered to by liberals with a taste for soap opera. Yet the thing keeps coming back—usually at election time—and the claims made for whichever Kennedy is the Kennedy of moment grow increasingly nauseating and outlandish. Is the Camelot buncombe ever to be lifted? Quite possibly not. Its current living legend, the Hon. Teddy, is only in the vestibule of middle age. If he does not suffer the cruel fate of his brothers, and if he lives out his years in the manner of Papa Joe and Mama Rose, he will be inspiring dithyrambs far into the twenty-first century. By then the brats will have come of age and Camelot will thus be carried on towards the twenty-second century. It is enough to make one yearn for the crack of doom.

What precisely is Camelot? If, like me, you are the sort who invariably feels a flutter of alarm extending onto nausea when confronted by, say, a Seventh Day Adventist, you may not

Public Nuisances

have pursued this question. Certainly you would never pursue it with one of Camelot's songsters. So allow me to intervene and bring forward one who has, the eminent James Mac-Gregor Burns, Ph.D. It is his view that Camelot is "an imperishable memory" for generations of Americans. Admittedly, that is not a pleasing thought. Yet in the course of my professional inquiries, I have now been obliged to steep myself in the lore of Camelot, and I must admit that Dr. Burns may be right. If so, we can do no less than thank him for the memories, for since the late 1950s he has dedicated his life to keeping the "imperishable memory" imperishable and inaccurate. He, too, is a fool for Camelot, a born fool in this case, and to read his slathering glorifications of the Kennedys is to be reminded of the heights that Bathhouse John Coughlin and Hinky Dink Kenna might have scaled had there been a Dr. Burns at large in Chicago's First Ward in the 1890s. As is the Camelotian custom, Dr. Burns' flame burns most brightly during election years; he is the proud author of *John Kennedy: A Political Profile* (1960) and *Edward Kennedy and the Camelot Legacy* (1976). Two volumes of kisses and curtsies.

But for the exertions of Dr. Burns, Mr. Schlesinger, and hundreds of lesser patriots, the aforementioned generations of Americans might actually forget the memory. Even worse, they might remember. For instance, they might remember the origins of Vietnam, the FBI's nocturnal knock on the door, the harassment of civil-rights leaders, the harassment of the press, the Vienna meeting with Khrushchev, the Bay of Pigs disaster, the ceaseless deception, the bellicose sonorities, the tumescent expectations, the cruel disappointments, and the ruinous decade that followed. It was a decade during which the loyal troopers of Camelot kept recasting "the memory," dropping episodes now discredited, adding episodes theretofore undreamt of, forever ensuring the memory's capacity to

216

The Hon. Teddy and the Camelot Buncombe

tantalize the eternal juvenile that frolics in the soul of every
ideologue.

Camelot is the pornography of American politics, always
promising the unattainable and rendering those who partici-
pate inflamed, infantile, and ludicrous. At its core is a mob
scene of delusions. Dr. Burns' maunderings in one book alone
(*Edward Kennedy and the Camelot Legacy*) convey Camelot's
idiot essence, as with vast solemnity he notifies us that Camelot's first prince "hated cant and sentimentality and blather."
John Kennedy "spoke with such force and gaiety and pointed-
ness, [that] he quickened the best impulses and spurred the
energies of his generation." But then, too, "there was a sense
of distance, of reserve, of separation"—and yet "engagement."
Camelot was "a special style": "of coolness and commitment,
of involvement and detachment." Ye Gods! It was "a brief and
shining moment." The room spins. Robert Kennedy was "the
existential hero." Spots appear before the eyes. Ted Kennedy
possessed "valiance of the highest order." The walls grow hair,
and still this clown will not shut off. . . . Kennedy I was "the
rhetorical radical," also "the policy liberal," then again "the
fiscal moderate," and, lest we forget, "the institutional conservative." Gangway! Every man for himself! There are some of
us who cannot swim.

Every year a journalist or a historian turns over another
rock, revealing ever more evidence of the fundamental impru-
dence and occasional stupidity of the Kennedy ménage. Still
the fabulists will not relent. You want biographies? We have
biographies. You want reminiscences? We have reminiscences. How about movies? Statuettes? T-shirts? Naturally there is
poetry, a full volume of the stuff commemorating JFK and
duly introduced by the indefatigable Arthur, who so loves life
that he read such wonders as the following and did not leap
out a window:

Public Nuisances

> He sort
> of embodied
> the air he sort
> of embodied the
> air where democracy
> stood tall, Jefferson
> and Robert Frost were
> his advisors, he sort
> of clearly gave evidence of
> wit and democracy. . . .*

In all the postwar period the only idolatry comparable to Camelot in tawdriness, senselessness, and longevity is the idolatry of Elvis Presley—though on this point Arthur would grow fussy. Camelot is devoted to the plain folk, to be sure, but even Camelot has its limits.

Think of it! Here we were, more than halfway into the twentieth century. It was the end of American innocence. For several decades the profs and the pundits had been assiduously delousing us of our accumulated jingoistic myths, and suddenly they turned and slammed down on us the most elaborate myth of all: the myth that a wheeler-dealer vulgarian, as rich as he was brutal, sired a family of archangels, fairy godmothers, and three genius sons who, despite private lives of sham and shallowness beyond belief, would somehow pull America—then the richest and freest nation on earth—out of a mysterious torpor and into an Augustan Age. How this would be accomplished has never been made clear, for the fabulists of Camelot spend very little time talking about ideas or policies. Rather, they devote most of their wind to elucidat-

---

* From "The Young President: March 1964," by John Tagliabue, in *Of Poetry and Power: Poems Occasioned by the Presidency and by the Death of John F. Kennedy*, edited by Erwin A. Glikes and Paul Schwaber, © 1964 by Basic Books, Inc., Publishers, New York. Reprinted by permission.

The Hon. Teddy and the Camelot Buncombe

ing the boys' mesmerizing personalities and their good intentions. The result has been some of the steamiest fiction in recent years. One sees it being wept over in sorority houses and imitated by third-rate homosexual novelists, but surely no serious student of American politics believes in it. After slogging through countless passages about the boys' struggles with destiny, their lighter sides and their darker sides, their courage, their passion, their goddamned "laconic wits," and so on, one wonders: is there any reality to the Camelot buncombe at all? Did Bobby Kennedy ever really exist? Does the Hon. Teddy exist today? After Mr. Marshall Frady described Bobby as "a protean revolutionary conscience [who] appeared in the form of a prince of the privileged orders," not only did Bobby slip from sight, but so did the country he allegedly "appeared in." Are we speaking of America or Ethiopia?

For years the Kennedys have been America's ceremonial Catholics, always turning up in the front pew of some stately cathedral whenever the occasion called. (What pious thoughts are on their minds when the cameras click, I have wondered.) Then they are off to the dance floors, the ski slopes, the Via Veneto, and the Champs Elysées—always the cameras are there. They show up in sad hovels in the Mississippi Delta, at celebrity tennis tournaments, at remote Eskimo villages. And then there are the untimely accidents—and, thank God, no cameras.

One looks at the mountains of books dedicated to spreading the Camelot buncombe, and one sees a Himalayan range of improbabilities: a legend of endless youth and exquisite romance spread by chelonian profs, a grandiose metaphor based on a Broadway musical and enthused over by the employees of Harvard. Scotch those snickers; there is more. The first Camelotian moments occurred in an hour of rare tranquility, yet Camelot's ministers saw only crisis. The rhetoric was menacing, the policies reckless; the aftermath was unreason at home, a huge international arms race abroad, and America's longest, most misdirected war. Nonetheless, to this day Camelot's faithful identify themselves adamantly and oleaginously as peacemakers.

In our time, no lie once set forth on the pages of the *New York Times* and welcomed in certain other august sanctums can ever be put to flight. According to one theory, times of decadence are times of artistic vigor, and it is on the artistic barrenness of our time that I have always staked my innocent hope that all is not so degenerate as meets the eye. But doubts are always alive. Is it possible that those elegant sophistries that preserve and protect the great lies of our time constitute a kind of renaissance? I think it is. Obviously it is no Florentine renaissance, but considering the creativity with which we guard our lies, I believe it is arguable that we are living through a renaissance of at least Weimarian distinction. And though we live in an age of little faith, no Arkansas hill ape swathed in rattlesnakes, full of strychnine, and hollering Mark 16:18 has exhibited greater faith than Arthur and Dr. Burns, sitting at their typewriters, devoutly pecking out their lamentations to fallen banners, "shining moments," and tribunes for "the dispossessed." This is not to say that Arthur's faith is without self-interest or remuneration. He has profited handsomely from the Camelot buncombe, but so have all the fabulists.

Rarely in history have the educated gone into such an encomiastic frenzy, and what inspires it? Kennedy I: three mediocre and dubious White House years; Kennedy II: less than a term as New York's junior senator and a stint at the Justice Department about which even the Camelotians grow coy; and now Kennedy III, with the most checkered career of all. Never

The Hon. Teddy and the Camelot Buncombe

has he held a job in the private sector. His early years in the Senate are remembered for carousals, amours, cronyism, and that inimitable yawn, which could be heard almost any time he was present in the Senate chamber. It was a loud, langourous yawn, even by Senate standards, and usually it was but an overture to even louder snores. Teddy was bounced from Harvard, laughed at during the public lives of his brothers, and bounced from a briefly held and poorly executed position in the Senate leadership. That last unhappy exit was occasioned by his sporadic indolence and one of the most appalling scandals in Senate history, the accident at Chappaquiddick and its ensuing fiasco. Nonetheless, in every presidential election since 1968 the wind tunnels of Camelot have whispered his name. How to explain it?

The answer is energy, the kind of excessive energy guaranteed by that lust for power and money that has always characterized the servitors of Camelot. One sees its magic in their organizational feats, their promotional accomplishments, and of course their polemical artistry. Never to be forgotten in this department was a great mélange of sociology, psychology, and what the ancients were wont to call malarky that Dr. Burns dumped on the Republic in 1976. The thing was obviously meant as a great silencer to undo all the accumulated allegations of Kennedy peccancy—those alluded to above and others too scabrous to mention in polite company. Throughout the Kennedy buncombe, this masterpiece has come to be recognized as the equivalent of the Hope Diamond. "The Kennedys," Dr. Burns assures us, "emerged from their own immigrant and religious heritage. . . . This special heritage helps explain, I think, why the Kennedys often seemed to break the rules. Joseph Kennedy's financial wheeling and dealing brought indignation and consternation to many a Back Bay breast. . . . As small boys the Kennedy brothers were not above occasional shoplifting. John Kennedy, according to a onetime teacher of his at Harvard, handed in a course paper that had clearly, or so the instructor thought, been supplied by the 'Widow's,' a firm selling papers to students (Jack denied it). Young Ted Kennedy's examination-evasion at Harvard was in part a way of coping with a somewhat alien culture." Why did the Nixon White House not think of this?

And so we are brought again to Kennedy III. What kind of president might he be? Based on his past achievements, one could see him taking his rightful place in presidential annals as a genial and goatish Grant. He has Grant's same doggedness,

The Hon. Teddy and the Camelot Buncombe

he squirmed through the same beginnings, he shares the same worm's eye view of the world. Teddy even shares Grant's famous hobby; though after a few shots Teddy generally sings—Grant merely snorted. Grant's sole aspiration in life was to teach mathematics at some Hayseed Harvard; only the ineptitude of other Union commanders brought him forward. At West Point no one could remember his name six weeks after he graduated. Early in his career, all that saved him from being court-martialed for drunkenness and neglect of duty was a well-timed retirement, an adroit move that came to be remembered as one of his few moments of cleverness. Everything else about the man was sheer tedium. He was a failure in all his pursuits save war, where he triumphed thanks to his always having a larger army and being ever willing to squander soldiers in some reckless way. When not in the height of battle, he showed little inclination to think and seems to have had no ideas of his own. In the end he was seen lying out in the Adirondacks furiously scribbling down his memoirs in hopes of saving his poor wife from a ravening mob of creditors. He finished four days before passing to his reward. True, the book is possibly the greatest American autobiography, but never to be forgotten is the fact that its author was a lifelong associate of unnumbered disasters, private and public. How does the Hon. Teddy differ? He is gayer, almost unbelievably more libidinous, and has an annual income of $450,000.

Few senators in this century rose from such otiose mediocrity. If it were not for the Kennedy millions and the enormous multitude of third-rate minds now inhabiting our public life and glad to have Teddy aboard, it is doubtful Teddy would ever have gotten to Washington. Certainly he would not have stayed. What Teddy would really have liked to do with his life is unknown. My guess is that there was a time when he wanted nothing more than to own a corner tavern somewhere in Boston, one with a jukebox that played "Happy Birthday" often. That his first ambition was not politics is certain. In his early years he had been jovially devoted to the hooch and the harp, both of which, along with fast driving and cuties, remain his only known cultural interests. Until his 1962 Senate race he totally ignored politics, voting only three times in his first sixteen opportunities, and those times his brother was on the ballot. These were crucial years in the Kennedys' rise to political eminence. There were many nights when the rooms of Hyannis Port filled with the smoke and the voices of Kennedy pols passionately machinating, but all that was ever heard from baby Teddy were a few bars of "My Wild Irish Rose" as he weaved toward his bedroom in the wee hours. I would like to have known him then; those were the happy days.

They ended all too suddenly the night his older brothers, President John and Attorney General Bobby, ambushed him and announced that he would be running for John's old Senate seat, then being kept warm by a family friend. No longer could he lounge about the big house by day and collect speeding tickets by night. Rarely was he free to sleep into the afternoon as had been his custom, and sometimes he had to be up by mid-morning. Shaking hands was not so bad, but public speaking could be dangerous, and debating his Democratic primary opponent, a veteran pol named Edward McCormack, was clearly painful. Every time these massacres took place, Teddy was battered mercilessly. Occasionally he was near tears, and toward the end of the campaign the merest mention of McCormack's name could make Teddy wince. Yet Kennedy money ($1.2 million) and a sympathy vote got him through, as it has in each of his subsequent campaigns.

Culturally, Teddy is a blank when not within shouting distance of a bartender. Even then he is not very interesting, though it must be said that he rarely forgets a good joke. When

The Hon. Teddy and the Camelot Buncombe

Teddy arrives in the White House it is going to take all the fabulists' creativity to present him to the world as anything other than one of those roisterous alums always seen cheering boozily at Notre Dame football games. What poet will they have him quoting, W. C. Fields? What musicians, artists, and metaphysicians will they be inviting to the White House, and how will Teddy treat them?

On his behalf it must be said that for many moons Teddy kept the fabulists of Camelot at arm's length. Perhaps it was their weird solemnity, perhaps their chaste admonitions. Whatever it was, he usually shunned them, and every time they mentioned him for the presidency he turned stone cold. In this he was well advised, for when they did get to him they nearly killed him off. Chappaquiddick was tragic, but the fabulists turned it into a farce that left every Kennedy-hater in the country beaming.

Maybe it was solely Teddy's idea to bring in the fabulists that week after the accident, maybe not, but it surely led to Camelot's most obnoxious moment of bathos, a speech of contrition to the people of Massachusetts. For a decade thereafter poor Teddy was viewed as a freak. Who can doubt that it would have gone better for him had he plainly admitted to having been on the sauce? Millions of Americans would have understood, prayed for Mary Jo Kopechne, and had done with it. Instead the fabulists had him suggesting mischief from demonic fates, speculating about a dark curse on the family, and begging an existential moment of insanity. Robert Kennedy might have carried it off, but not a man of Teddy's essential bovinity. To have this big doll of a man intoning Camelotian sonorities when his guilt was so unmistakable was to mark him down as an ass for life. There sat two hundred pounds of woebegone *Playboy* philosophy declaring: "It has been written that a man does what he must, in spite of personal conse-

quences, in spite of obstacles and dangers and pressures. . . .
that is the basis of all human morality. . . . The stories of past
courage cannot supply courage itself. For this each man must
look into his own soul. I pray that I can have the courage to
make the right decision," etc., etc., *ad nauseam*.

Was the corrupting influence of Camelot ever more obvious? Was its dreamy amorality ever more apparent? There was
a fatal automobile accident. Teddy fled the scene and failed to
report the accident. In response the fabulists roll up their
sleeves, spit on their hands, and transform the sordid event
into romance, an inscrutable mystery, a personal triumph,
another "shining moment." The Hon. Teddy lectures the citizenry on morality and the need for prayer. He invokes the
names of fallen Kennedys and speculates on man's fate. There
is a homiletic outburst about courage and honor, two virtues
conspicuously lacking in his recent behavior. Camelot's insistence on delusion was never more patent, and the whole
claque joined in. Arthur informed America that "with Chappaquiddick the iron went into Edward Kennedy's soul." Richard J. Walton speculated that "perhaps Chappaquiddick was
fate's final test, one that would destroy him or prove him."
And it was after Chappaquiddick that the fabulous Dr. Burns
remarked on Teddy's "valiance of the highest order." What is
their point? That automobile accidents are the testing ground
for presidential greatness? That Chappaquiddick is the Camelotian equivalent of the playing fields of Eton? That this fatal
botch made Teddy a better person?

Of all the Kennedys, the Hon. Teddy is the least appropriate
candidate for the Camelot purple. He has no elegance, no
romance, no vision, and only the most pedestrian intelligence.
After Chappaquiddick he got to work in the Senate, but of all
the liberals he has shown the least capacity to learn from the
past. In a time of doubt about the collectivist nostrums, he

The Hon. Teddy and the Camelot Buncombe

hollers for the most dubious and expensive statist policy of all, nationalized health care. The whole country resounds with doubts about bureaucracy's beadledom and the state's infringements on personal liberty, and Teddy wants to extend the genius of the postal service and the regulatory agencies into ever more areas of American life.

In brief and in sum, Teddy will give the twentieth century a Grant. Grant recklessly heaved Union troops at his problems; Teddy heaves money and coercive laws. Grant was seedier, but then Teddy is surrounded by aides for every occasion. Moreover, he has the fabulists to see to it that when memoir time comes Teddy writes claptrap.

26

Henry Kissinger:
Metternich Flummoxed

$\mathbf{M}$ANY BELIEVE that what the learned and immensely complicated Dr. Henry Kissinger really thinks of it all would make an engrossing tale. Surely he has seen many marvels: stormtroopers in old Fürth, crestfallen stormtroopers in Allied Occupied Germany; Harvard; the Council on Foreign Relations; and, in the fullness of time, the White House—in whose mess he fattened so prodigiously that he became a hazard to revolving doors and a challenge to Air Force One. Dr. Kissinger has seen all this and more: he has seen the doe-eyed Daniel Ellsberg whipped into a shameful anti-Communist frenzy, and he has had wet kisses planted on both his cheeks by Egypt's President Anwar El-Sadat. There were clandestine missions to Paris, Moscow, Peking, and to the Georgetown quarters of the inscrutable Miss Barbara Howar. All around the world he has passed *le sel et le poivre* to our era's greatest notables. Yet he was a scholar, one with a world view, and when he articulated that view, snatches of Wagner could be heard, occasionally even the *Missa Solemnis*. Surely behind today's drollery and politesse stands a man who could disclose some astounding truths. I doubt it.

The author of *A World Restored* and *The Necessity for Choice* knew something once, but once is not enough. One does not sweat and smile, turning one's whole life into a media event, and return with one's *Weltanschauung* intellectually in blossom. It is a melancholy but well-researched truth that modern America confers celebrity and power most frequently on poseurs, quacks, and halfwits. The biography of Dr. Kissinger is the chronicle of how Bismarck was made presentable to Shirley MacLaine and David Susskind, how Metternich was made comprehensible to Walter Cronkite, and how Castlereagh was transformed into a mercurial buffoon. In the end such acts grow tedious. Henry's Spenglerian-Hegelian whimwham may make Georgetown debutantes weep, but grown-ups become restless.

Must public life as it is lived today stultify all who populate it? Obviously many of our national worthies are simply jackasses. They did not have to detune their cerebrums and take to amphetamines to render themselves acceptable to *People* magazine or to network television. Their fevered asininity was with them at birth. But Heinze Alfred Kissinger was different. Born with a brain and the good sense to use it, he, in his salad days, had held to sound ideas, however ploddingly expressed. He saw the Marxist conjurers for the cutthroat plunderers they were and always must be. He warned that they would keep the world in a pother, and that there are in life dilemmas invincibly resistant to the therapies of social science. He recognized the Soviets as a tribe of pathological liars, and the world's meliorists made him laugh. Dr. Kissinger found wisdom in history and philosophy, and throughout the 1950s and most of the 1960s he propounded sensible suggestions for scotching the Soviets' mischief. How many other public persons could claim as much?

But Dr. Kissinger liked to eat. From the day he graduated from Harvard, Henry relished nothing so much as vichyssoise with the greats, and if the greats tended to drone on about palpable nonsense, so what? Henry could always concentrate on the Oysters Rockefeller or the Corton Charlemagne. It was to Henry's immense benefit that when he arrived in Washington prandial anthropology had already become a matter of vast consequence in our capital's political struggles. Upon leaving government eight years later he was fifty pounds too much for his shoes. Numerous chins overwhelmed the knot in his tie, and cardiologists all over the eastern seaboard were sending him their business cards. All Washington idolized him, and those who had worked for him either were keeping their mouths shut or filing law suits against him. His smiling presence had become as ubiquitous as Cubans in Africa, Soviet naval vessels in the Mediterranean Sea or the Indian Ocean, Red flags in Southeast Asia, and "Yankee-cough-up" diatribes at the UN. How did he accomplish all this? How had Henry become the most celebrated secretary of state in modern times and the least effective? He understood the complexity of modern American public life.

Henry had bamboozled practically everyone in our nation's capital and with a style transcending FDR at the height of his powers. Foreign dignitaries collected Kissingerian whoppers as proof of their country's geopolitical significance. Native Washingtonians took his dissemblings as manifestations of his debonair brilliance. In a city devoted to deception Henry came to be its most warmly esteemed artist of flimflam. Washingtonians reverenced his charms, and it is suggestive of the complicated minds that flourish along the Potomac that many of them actually grew to trust him. One columnist wrote a sagacious appraisal of the man, advancing the difficult proposition that Henry was: (a) one of the town's most notorious liars and (b) a uniquely trusted world figure. How can such contradictory claptrap issue from a stalwart of America's illustrious fourth estate? Probably he is a genius: one of those giants of modern America who perceive uncommon wisdom, liberality, and farsightedness in that which less sophisticated observers dismiss as mere trumpery, plausible but hollow beyond measure.

Washington is a city abundant with such giants, and one can never come to appreciate the sad stultification of Henry without understanding their mores and folkways. Some of the giants, naturally enough, are pols and bureaucratic mullahs, but many are above the fray. Some are journalists, well known to the American public thanks to the frequency with which they award each other TV appearances and prizes for journalistic daring. Others are lawyers, or super-lawyers as the muckrakers are given to calling them. These number into the hundreds, for there are more lawyers per square foot in Washington than in Allenwood, Pennsylvania; Danbury, Connecticut; or Lompoc, California. Still others are simple intellectuals, do-good lobbyists, militant heiresses, respected interior decorators, and people who seem to do nothing but attend Washington cocktail parties—a very solemn function indeed, as our embattled president has discovered. The Wonderboy and his down-home clods had hardly unloaded their mules at Union Station when the *Washington Post's* learned Sally Quinn delivered up a brisk treatise on the importance of the Washington cocktail party to American statecraft. It was but the first of many public-spirited attempts to inform the Wonderboy of the serious nature of highballpolitik. Yet the Baptist yokel is untutorable; his assistant presidents remain locked in the White House, available only for special appearances at

stock-car races and cow-chip heaves. It has been estimated that
for every cocktail party the administration has failed to attend
one hundred thousand votes have been lost nationwide, along
with choice pieces of legislation. The patriots at Sans Souci
have thrown up their hands.

Washington's giants compose a kind of informal oligarchy
duly overseeing power and celebrity throughout the city and
defining the various formulae for acceptable style. Many are
the kind of people given to describing themselves as compassionate, decent, and liberal, but that is not to imply that they
are ideologues. Rather they are drawn together by a very modern sophistication, a worldly sensibility celebrating life and
success and survival despite nearly constant harassment from
the silent majority, the Chamber of Commerce, and all those
petty people given to calling themselves "tax-paying Americans." The tawdry celebration of success, particularly financial success, has for decades been one of the less appealing
aspects of American life, but the glorification of success by
Washingtonians is a world removed from the bourgeois orgies
of, say, the Rotary. In Washington one almost never mentions
money, at least one never mentions the act of amassing
money. Instead one celebrates the spending of it and that mysterious ontological state called fame.

At least since the palmy days of Camelot it has been an article of dogma in Washington that "the unpublicized life is not
worth living," and so the giants are all in very thick with what
the wretched Agnew was wont to call "the media." And why
not? There are giants in the media too, and anyway one has to
do one's part to keep the evening news interesting and the
newsweeklies *au courant*. Hence the giants have sacrificed
much of their own privacy to allow the camera just a peek.
"Oh well," one hears a glum Professor Arthur Schlesinger, Jr.,

mutter as he drags his fully clothed bulk from yet another Kennedy swimming pool, "if it will get decency and enlightened liberalism a favorable word in *Time* or a picture in *Town and Country*, it's worth it." Other occasions also receive the glare of publicity: nickle-dime charitable affairs at Hickory Hill, fund-raising dinners for various far-off legal defense funds, and concerts at the famed Kennedy Center for the Performing Arts—one of America's few examples of Middle-Mussolini architecture. Here the giants' perennial smiles are put to a most exacting trial, for there is something about an evening of Brahms or Schumann that apparently roils the bowels of a fundamental sap—"why does it have to be so loud?" I have actually been to the Kennedy Center during an evening of Beethoven and can personally testify to having heard the following

233

observations: "Ethel, there was something chillingly Naziish about that piece . . . do you think Beethoven was very happy? . . . People didn't eat very well in those days."

Henry firmly believed—and with justification—that today in America one cannot get one's policies accepted without comforting these asses, and so he set out to conquer Georgetown. It was an audacious course, for the cachet of a Harvard prof loses everything when the prof is in the employment of the hellish Nixon—which Henry was. Yet in one of the quieter passages of his frequently quoted undergraduate thesis Henry had noted that: "Life involves suffering and transitoriness. No person can choose his age or the condition of his time. . . . The generation of Buchenwald and the Siberian labor-camps cannot talk with the same optimism as its fathers. The bliss of Dante has been lost in our civilization." And so he trudged off to dinner at the Alsops, drinks at the Harrimans, and those intimate evenings with Barbara Howar. Perhaps these hours with Barbara were the cruelest of all. The North Vietnamese were then flummoxing his every scheme, the Soviets had him by the short hairs, the world seemed alive with protesting adolescents, and poor Henry had to spend whole evenings listening to a nincompoop talk of her mother. Nevertheless there was news value in these trysts, and, according to Henry's grand strategy, he needed the ink.

By day he hummed through the White House, the most obsequious flatterer ever imagined in this democratic Republic. Richard Nixon had never seen such violent devotion. They planned geopolitical strategy together, conceptualized together, tapped telephones together. In time they even prayed together. Yet by night he dined and disported with the giants of the town. For the giants these were frightening years. Nixon was in JFK's bathtub, he was populating Washington with what appeared to be Jaycees from some weird midwestern state, and *Rolling Stone* had revealed that he planned to cancel the 1972 presidential elections, which meant the conventions too, and maybe even the inaugural ball. White House gossip had practically evaporated, there being few giants willing to claim a source in Nixon's administration, and the resulting sense of emptiness and powerlessness made their gatherings ever more subdued and melancholy. Into all this woe came Henry, amusing, stimulating, and now obligatory. He kept the giants alive.

There they would sit in one of their glittering town houses, a manse now made sad by the Nixon madness. Nervously they would exchange ominous morsels about the fiend's latest deviltry. Henry's arrival—always dramatically late—would send a rush of relief through the room. I can see him now centered in a halo of anxious faces. Solemnly he reports the day's geopolitical developments, as mounds of canapés disappear into the undulating folds of his face. A hush of grandeur settles about the erstwhile prof as he heaves off sizzling *bons mots* and follows up with sobering Hegelian vaporings. An agitated Georgetown dowager reports her young nephew's most current judgment on the war. A fashion designer of intellectual mien inquires about Nixon's mental health. And all the assembled geniuses bask in the realization that only in Washington is such a gathering of "the best, the truly best in every field" possible. Gad! How Henry's mind must have wandered. Surely there were times when, as the saps gibbered fervently, a lonely Dr. Kissinger entertained errant thoughts, quietly computing to himself how many quarts of cement might seal off his garrulous hostess' mouth or speculating on how often the mansion's chief domestic must needs inspect her mistress' bathrooms for unflushed toilets. Considering the numbing hours Henry spent massaging such dreary oafs, it is amazing that he never became a drunk or a narcoleptic.

Public Nuisances

Instead he became Washington's premier attraction, and even out of office his mere presence can confer immortality upon a dinner party or an opening night. Yet, though cocktail parties are a crucial political arena in the higher reaches of modern America, they apparently do not loom so large internationally. Henry may have slayed those who write for the "Style" section of the *Washington Post*, but the North Vietnamese do not seem to have made cocktail parties a theater of operations. The Soviets, admittedly, are assiduous cocktail-party participants, but history has shown that for the loyal Soviet citizen the cocktail party is merely an opportunity to get oneself raucously sozzled and one's capitalist guest sick. How much dreadful vodka poor Henry consumed while convincing the wary Bolsheviki of détente's benefits will remain a mystery until some strenuous prof undertakes the definitive biography; but no one capable of reading a newspaper in the late seventies can believe that the time Henry spent boozing with them sweetened them up. America has as many morons as the next country, but by the late 1970s only George McGovern remained adamantine in proclaiming the peaceful aspirations of Ivan the Terrible's heirs.

Détente came to be the centerpiece of Henry's foreign policy, and in humbug and hollowness it was perfectly tailored for the meaninglessness of the 1970s. Détente was catnip for the catnip-loving greats of the Washington Establishment; its sophistry and obfuscation were perfectly congenial to their insulationist mentality. But détente was raw meat for the Comrades, and its consequences must have made our Henry a stupendously derisory figure in their eyes.

The Comrades ignored Henry's understanding of détente from the start. As Henry understood it, Papa Brezhnev's first move would be to call off the North Vietnamese. In point of fact he energetically set about fortifying their arsenals. He then commenced the most massive military build-up of all time, and soon his colleagues were raising hell throughout Africa and the Middle East. In 1973 Brezhnev journeyed to Prague to assure an assemblage of Marxist-Leninist apes that "we are achieving with détente what our predecessors have been unable to achieve using the mailed fist." Full of progressive vision he went on to report that "we have been able to accomplish more in a short time with détente than was done for years pursuing a confrontation policy with NATO. . . . Trust us, comrades, for by 1985, as a consequence of what we are now achieving with détente, we will have achieved most of our objectives in Western Europe. We will have consolidated our position. We will have improved our economy. And a decisive shift in the correlation of forces will be such that, come 1985, we will be able to extend our will wherever we need to." It was one of those historic moments that so easily lend themselves to willful misinterpretation by anti-Communist Neanderthals, and Henry must have winced. But only the *Boston Globe*, *National Review*, and *The American Spectator* reported the speech. Back in Washington it was cocktails as usual; détente had survived.

In terms of traditional American foreign policy goals of security and freedom of action, détente was a catastrophe, but in Henry's complicated political calculation it was a splendid triumph. By 1974 the Soviets' Cuban mercenaries were crawling all over Africa, but 1974 was also the year in which Henry was acclaimed "the greatest person in the world today" by the callipygian contestants of the Miss Universe pageant. No other secretary of state had ever known such distinction.

The rapidity and thoroughness with which Henry was taken in by the mediocrity and bunkum of our Alexandrian Age should give every admirer of intellect cause for unease. Obviously Henry needed something more than intelligence and bromo-seltzer to become a modern Metternich. He needed sound character. Henry's admirers attempt to explain away his artifice and appeasement by reminding us of his belief in the decline of the West and his skepticism about the strengths and uses of democratic politics. I began as one of Henry's admirers, but as with so many other claims made for him, this claim withers under scrutiny. The West may be in decline, but the East is in stagnation, and it is governed by large numbers of obvious meatheads. Anyway, from July 1975 to February 1976 Henry was given a vivid demonstration of democracy's vitality when his own UN ambassador roused Americans to resist the pecksniffery of the UN's tinpot despotisms. Henry contrived to have Mr. Moynihan fired, but by this time Mr. Moynihan could have run successfully for elected office from any of half a dozen states. Had Henry been a man of sound character he might have forthrightly taken his case to the citizenry beyond Washington; he might have resisted the corruptions of that Alexandrian stew along the Potomac; and he might have spared us his melodramatic bellowings and blubberings. But then, no one doubts that Aleksandr Solzhenitsyn is buoyed by strong character, and when he came to Washington not even Jerry Ford would dine with him. Had Dr. Kissinger come to Washington with the character of a Solzhenitsyn he might have starved to death.

27

Har Har, A Manifesto

THE MAN: his eyes roving, his sweaty hand yearning for another transient flesh-pressing, his head full of what the dispassionate observer recognizes instantly as hallucinations. Our subject's dress is extraordinary, a catastrophic confrontation between the garish and the vaguely Churchillian. He puts one in mind of a pallbearer at a homosexual funeral. A maniacal eagerness marks his every gesture. He grins: "Hi, I'm running for president. Call me Birch, not Senator."

THE WOMAN: her eyes darting to the left and the right, her face handsome enough, but her forehead suggestive of a knee. Her body lumbers beneath a caparison of contemporary elegance; she is loudly nonviolent, but the clothes she wears bespeak the military: epaulets, belts, many pockets, and zippers. Khaki is her favored color. She speaks in slogans, and what she intones is not sunny. When she was a little girl she strangled the family cat.

Ladies and gentlemen, I give you two gifted Americans: the first, an American senator hotly pursuing destiny's call; the second, a women's liberationist dutifully earning a handsome

Public Nuisances

living for herself and a cute wire-haired terrier. These are only two specimens of the many remarkable Americans who emerged in the 1960s and 1970s, intent on enlightening us, improving us, and in general having a gorgeous time of it. They are sober, assiduous, and abounding with advanced ideas. They tour the nation speaking on TV shows, on college campuses, and at prandial atrocities. They deliver teary and triumphant testimonials to each other, grant interviews, and even write books. Some take to the barricades, such as they are these days. Some carry placards in front of the house where Coolidge slept. These are the celebrities of American public life. If it were not for their exertions America would have ten times more poor people, twenty times more innocent prison inmates, and every American woman would either be chained to the bed or to the kitchen sink. A fundamentalist president, possibly from Georgia, would tyrannize us. The Klan would be running the nation's mental-health associations and illiteracy would be a real problem. Without the rise of these celebs devoted to the public interest there would be no stopping the Chamber of Commerce.

So we are lead to believe, but I grow skeptical. To me these busybodies are as moronic a mob of louts as has ever been at large in any civilized country since the dawn of Christendom. Yet it is the current American custom to urge that the public grant them a respectful hearing and a serious rebuttal. It is appalling. Some notions parading around the Republic today are so preposterous and sniveling that to accord them careful analysis and courteous rejoinder is to accord them a dignity that is as undeserved as it is injurious to public morals.

Truth to tell, those who bawl for women's "liberation," homosexual "rights," black nationalism, populism, and the prohibition of tobacco in public places are charlatans whose very causes are generally misnomers. The rights of women and homosexuals are practically indistinguishable from the rights of the average Americano, and when these haranguers ask for something more they are asking for privileges. If they cannot bear the burden of those privileges too bad for them. The sophistries they spin are unworthy of more than a horselaugh. Ritualistic liberals might take them seriously, but there is no compelling reason for the civilized minority to corrupt ratiocination by hearing them out and replying soberly.

Whoever heard of discussing immunology with a peripatetic snake-oil salesman? And why should I discuss politics or history with some lunatic woman whose thesis is that rape has, since Adam, been the fundamental nexus between man and woman? That particular hallucination set many minds to pondering in 1975 and it was considered infra dig. to chortle.

Over the years many eminent writers of sound mind and sturdy constitution have lectured me on the impropriety of ridiculing the ridiculous. How absurd. They withdraw to their book-lined lairs, kiss their pictures of Matthew Arnold, and essay learned and rigorous rejoinders to the fanatics of the moment. How wasteful. Such tracts are often engaging and occasionally even edifying, but I suspect their impact on the public discourse is rarely more influential than the State of the Union message or a speech from Rosalynn Carter.

What the sober-minded always neglect is the doleful fact that the proponents of mischief and nonsense are under no obligation to respond to intelligent criticism. In fact, if the past decade or so is any guide, it is clear that they resent it and hide from it. I never heard of William Kunstler taking up the challenge of the late Alexander Bickel nor do I expect I ever will. Will Ralph Nader ever consider the intelligent essays of Irving Kristol? The thing is impossible to imagine. Why waste wind on such a lout? Ridicule him and spare the courtesies.

What the media does with them is even more absurd.

Public Nuisances

When a television station's public affairs department decides to take up some burning issue it is the custom to bring in the weirdest ultraist not yet behind bars and to encourage him to fuss and rage and spin yarns that might be considered wild even by the standards of a practicing sociologist. In the 1960s almost never was civil rights discussed by peaceful, intelligent minds. Instead the TV networks had a habit of latching on to some obscure fuliginous lunatic and balancing him off with a demented kleagle or a kinky anthropologist, steeped in the lore of Nordic supremacy and hankering for women's lingerie. I consider it a statement of fact that half the extremist organizations in the country would have long ago gone bankrupt and dissolved if it were not for local broadcasting media's need for their appearances on public-affairs broadcasts. I personally know a black militant who was kept so busy during the early 1970s that he had to give up his teaching position at a small Indiana college. Eventually he came to believe that the celebrity television gave him was part of a honky plot to damage his career and his health. He went to work for a bank. Far from giving truth a chance to triumph, the impressarios of dialogue merely contribute to the perpetuation of extremism. America's chief inducements to the careers of charlatans and of malcontents are talk shows and the college lecture circuit. Where else could aging radicals, John Dean, and astrologers do so well?

I do not mean to denigrate serious scholarship, nor do I intend to condemn an occasional serious polemic against some idiotic enthusiasm. I do believe that a great deal of serious polemicism can be put down as wasted breath and—what is worse—delusion. Serious replies to the canards heaved up by the women of the fevered brow are no doubt useful and desirable, but they are generally useful only to those who already know what is what or to those presently in transit. When they lend dignity to an idiotic position or when they perpetuate the misconception that idiots and mischievous zealots are fetched by reason, serious replies themselves become mischievous, for they send armies of bright and civilized persons off into the archives to meditate on hokum while leaving the levers of power to the cranks.

Today the vast majority of panaceas for reform and justice so-called are, in a word, foolish. What is more they are the enthusiasms of profoundly committed fools. No amount of careful argumentation is going to disabuse these fools of their moonshine. Some analysis may clarify the issues and even offer a passing opportunity for enlightenment, but that is about it. Egalitarianism is a doctrine so bashed and battered by learned syllogisms that it is, intellectually speaking, a basket case. Yet today it rides high, and those who have pummeled it with their logic and learning are back in their libraries pondering how a world that has witnessed the likes of Mother Teresa of Calcutta, and Charles Manson, Churchill, and Chamberlain can still wobble at the thought that we are all easily and duly folded into cookie molds. They are stumped. They are prayerful. They wonder how next to battle this idiotic and baneful idea. My suggestion is that they roll up their sleeves, spit on their hands, and ridicule the rascals who afflict us.

Scholarship is important, serious analysis of contemporary problems is necessary, but when contemporary problems reek with foolishness and purposive foolishness at that, the only way to scotch the rascals is to pull off their vestments and expose their monkeyshines. Moreover, in a world full of influenza, and presidential primaries, it is about the only harmless amusement left.

Still the sober-minded resist, admonishing that were they to give themselves over to lampooning the eminently lampoonable the plain folk of the Republic would conclude that there exists no serious core of values for society to defend. A cal-

umny against the plain folk, I reply, and a malversation
against the record. It was not the AFL–CIO and the Knights of
Pythias that accorded solemnity to the cause of the militant
pederasts or to the sponsors of Alice Doesn't Day, that memorable day in 1975 when the presidium of the women's mob ordered all self-respecting women to sulk. This spoonery can be
chalked up to the intelligentsia and the urban sophisticates.
They are the people who pondered the absurdities of the last
two decades; the feeble-minded amongst them capitulating to
and countenancing obvious flapdoodle, while the sober-minded
withdrew to the archives and composed their tracts. The tracts
have devastated every absurd claim. Today we can honestly
say that women's liberation and homosexual liberation have
ushered in not one intelligent or useful idea. Yet the flyblown
ideas endure and menace our freedom through legal atrocities
like affirmative action. It was not the plain folk who were corrupted or hoodwinked. They jeered and hooted at every asinine notion. When they heard of respected thinkers meditat-
ing on these asinine ideas they were astonished. When the
asinine ideas became law they were discouraged. Now they are
low; they need a boost.

I prescribe ridicule. It is an equitable response to the likes of
Ralph Nader or Betty Friedan. It is a soothing emollient for
our peculiarly troubled national spirit. Ridicule does not ele-
vate nonsense to any higher level than that at which it is emit-
ted. It is entertaining and far more edifying to the public discourse than the facile dissimulations now rampant there.
Ridicule is the compliment lively intelligence pays to jackass-
ery. It is a national treasure certified by Mark Twain, beloved
by millions, and eschewed only at great peril. Use it wisely and
learn from it.

Index

Index

Index